LawExpress
ENVIRONMENTAL LAW

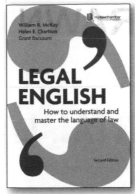

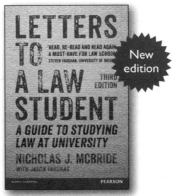

Law Express

ENVIRONMENTAL LAW

2nd edition

Simon Sneddon
University of Northampton

PEARSON

Harlow, England • London • New York • Boston • San Francisco • Toronto • Sydney • Auckland • Singapore • Hong Kong
Tokyo • Seoul • Taipei • New Delhi • Cape Town • São Paulo • Mexico City • Madrid • Amsterdam • Munich • Paris • Milan

Pearson Education Limited
Edinburgh Gate
Harlow CM20 2JE
United Kingdom
Tel: +44 (0)1279 623623
Web: www.pearson.com/uk

First published 2013 (print and electronic)
Second edition published 2015 (print and electronic)

ISBN: 978-1-292-01291-9 (print)
    978-1-292-01339-8 (PDF)
    978-1-292-01814-0 (ePub)
    978-1-292-01309-1 (eText)

British Library Cataloguing-in-Publication Data
A catalogue record for the print edition is available from the British Library

Library of Congress Cataloging-in-Publication Data
A catalog record for the print edition is available from the Library of Congress

10 9 8 7 6 5 4 3 2 1
18 17 16 15 14

Print edition typeset in 10/12pt Helvetica Neue LT Std by 35
Print edition printed and bound in Malaysia (CTP-PPSB)

NOTE THAT ANY PAGE CROSS REFERENCES REFER TO THE PRINT EDITION

Contents

Supporting resources

Visit the Law Express series Companion Website at **www.pearsoned.co.uk/lawexpress** to find valuable student learning material including:

- A **study plan** test to assess how well you know the subject before you begin your revision, now broken down into targeted study units
- Interactive **quizzes** with a variety of question types to test your knowledge of the main points from each chapter of the book
- Further **examination questions** and guidelines for answering them
- Interactive **flashcards** to help you revise the main terms and cases
- Printable versions of the **topic maps** and **checklists**
- **'You be the marker'** allows you to see exam questions and answers from the perspective of the examiner and includes notes on how an answer might be marked
- **Podcasts** provide point-by-point instruction on how to answer a common exam question

Also: The companion website provides the following features:

- Search tool to help locate specific items of content
- E-mail results and profile tools to send results of quizzes to instructors
- Online help and support to assist with website usage and troubleshooting

For more information please contact your local Pearson Education sales representative or visit **www.pearsoned.co.uk/lawexpress**

Acknowledgements

There are many people who I would like to thank for their support and assistance in producing this text. Thanks first of all to Katie, for always being there for me. Thanks also to all of the anonymous reviewers for their useful and well-judged feedback. Finally, thanks to my editor, Christine Statham, without whose patience and expertise this would have progressed little further than a collection of loose ideas.

Simon Sneddon
University of Northampton

Publisher's acknowledgements

Our thanks go to all reviewers who contributed to the development of this text, including students who participated in research and focus groups which helped to shape the series format.

Introduction

Welcome to environmental law! Although many of the concepts that underpin environmental law have been established for a long time, many people still think of it as a relatively new topic. There are also links between environmental law in its broadest sense and many other areas of law and policy, from housing to transport to energy to waste. Environmental law also impacts, and is impacted on, by developments in scientific understanding of problems, as well as wider socio-economic issues, both locally and internationally. My students are made aware that there is very little (if anything) that they do from before they are born to after they die that is not covered in one respect or another by environmental law. However, as your own course will tell you, and this guide will reiterate, what we mean when we talk about environmental law as an academic discipline is considerably narrower in scope.

There are some specific issues that students face when trying to answer questions on environmental law and, in the main, these tend to be different for problem and essay questions. There are common problems that come up, for example the difficulties that emerge when entire areas of environmental law are amended – such as happened with the passage of the Environmental Permitting (England and Wales) Regulations 2010 and the Localism Act 2011.

There are also specific issues that may occur in relation to different types of question. For problem questions, the main issues hinge around knowing which aspects of the scenario are relevant to the specific aspects of environmental law that the question is posing. For example, a problem question on planning law could overlap with environmental permitting, habitat protection, issues of enforcement and so on. Other areas of potential problem include the application of concepts and principles of environmental law to a specific scenario. For example, relating sustainable development to a problem question on waste management.

For essay questions, the main issue which causes problems for some students is the use of case law to illustrate the answer. In some ways, this is a generic issue, but it is exacerbated in environmental law where a case may have been decided on issues of interpretation or application of relatively new and emerging principles.

Students generally do reasonably well in assessments in this topic area, although their chances of success rise dramatically in direct correlation to their attendance and participation in lectures, seminars and tutorials, not to mention using the recommended textbook! The point is that this guide is not intended to be a replacement for any of those things – it will complement them, and is designed specifically as an *aide-mémoire*.

📖 REVISION NOTE

Make sure you are aware of up-to-date changes in legislation, as several areas of environmental law are in flux at the moment.

Be careful of overlapping areas of law – both within the environmental law area and between environmental and other types of law – and make sure you shape your answer around the focus of the question. Also, when revising with cases that involve environmental and non-environmental areas of law, be careful to focus on the relevant aspects of the judgment.

Before you begin, you can use the study plan available on the companion website to assess how well you know the material in this book and identify the areas where you may want to focus your revision.

Guided tour

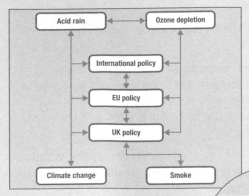

Topic maps – Visual guides highlight key subject areas and facilitate easy navigation through the chapter. Download them from the companion website to pin on your wall or add to your revision notes.

Revision checklists – How well do you know each topic? Use these to identify essential points you should know for your exams. But don't panic if you don't know them all – The chapters will help you revise each point to ensure you are fully prepared. Print the checklists off the companion website and track your revision progress!

Revision checklist

Essential points you should know:

☐ How acid rain happens, and how internatio

☐ What ozone layer depletion is, and how int

☐ The causes (and cures) of climate change

☐ What UK policy and legislation are doing

Sample questions with answer guidelines – Practice makes perfect! Read the question at the start of each chapter and consider how you would answer it. Guidance on structuring strong answers is provided at the end of the chapter. Try out additional sample questions online.

▪ Sample question

Could you answer this question? Below is a typical problem question that could arise on this topic. Guidelines on answering the question are included at the end of this chapter, whilst a sample essay question and guidance on tackling it can be found on the companion website.

Assessment advice – Not sure how best to tackle a problem or essay question? Wondering what you may be asked? Use the assessment advice to identify the ways in which a subject may be examined and how to apply your knowledge effectively.

ASSESSMENT ADVICE

Water pollution could easily form the whole of an essay or problem question, or part of a wider question.

Essay questions

A common theme for essay questions would be to ask you to evaluate the impact of Directive 2000/60/EC ('the Water Framework Directive') on the pollution control regime in the EU. You should watch out for the implementation dates of the daughter directives.

Key definitions – Make sure you understand essential legal terms. Use the flashcards online to test your recall!

KEY DEFINITION: Emissions trading (FCCC, 2011, Art. 17)

Countries with emission units to spare – emissions permitted them but not 'used' – can sell this excess capacity to countries that are over their targets. Carbon, for example, is now tracked and traded like any other commodity.

Key cases and statutes
– Identify and review the
important elements of the
essential cases and statutes
you will need to know for your
exams.

KEY STATUTE
Article 4, Directive 2008
(1) The following waste h
    management legislatio
    (a) prevention;
    (b) preparing for re
    (c) recycling;

KEY CASE
Alphacell v Woodward [1972] AC 824
Concerning: intention; pollution; rivers; strict liability; causing

Facts

Polluting matter entered a river from settling tanks as a result of blockage of a pump
strainer by 'brambles ferns and leaves'. The tanks had been inspected prior to the
overflow and found to be working properly.

Make your answer stand out – This
feature illustrates sources of further thinking
and debate where you can maximise your
marks. Use them to really impress your
examiners!

✓   Make your answer stand out

There have been some discussions recently about the lack of certainty surrounding
'material change of use'. See, for example, Humphreys (2011), who finishes by saying,
'After over 60 years of the present concept of "development", it is surely time for
clarity.' Use this to impress the examiners by discussing whether 'material change of
use' ought to still be 'a question of fact and degree in every case' or whether it should
be defined by statute.

Exam tips – Feeling the pressure? These
boxes indicate how you can improve your
exam performance when it really counts.

🖉 EXAM TIP

There is often talk of measures being introduced without proper understanding of their
consequences. The landfill tax, for example, is regularly linked to an increase in illegal
fly-tipping. Look at the arguments put forward by Pocklington and Pocklington (1998)
in the early days of the tax and, more recently, Bennett (2010).

Revision notes – Get guidance for effective
revision. These boxes highlight related
points and areas of overlap in the subject,
or areas where your course might adopt a
particular approach that you should check
with your course tutor.

📖 REVISION NOTE

One practical embodiment of the precautionary principle is illustrated in Chapter 5
(on planning) and Chapter 6 (on environmental permitting) as environmental impact
assessments, which should be considered alongside the theory.

Don't be tempted to . . . – This feature
underlines areas where students most often
trip up in exams. Use them to spot common
pitfalls and avoid losing marks.

❗ Don't be tempted to . . .

Don't assume that even with widespread international agreement on the scientific
background to climate change, there will be consensus as to how to tackle it. There is
a clear divide between the approaches that tend to be favoured by developing nations
(especially China, Brazil and India) and the approaches favoured in the West.
Remember that this is a highly contentious political issue, as well as a legal one.

Read to impress – Focus on these carefully
selected sources to extend your knowledge,
deepen your understanding, and earn better
marks in coursework as well as in exams.

READ TO IMPRESS

Barham, S. and Cockrell, C. (2011) ECJ decision on ETS could have serious impact, *LLID* 28 Jan, 7

Bell, S. McGillivray, D. and Pedersen, O. (2013) *Environmental Law*, 8th Edn. Oxford: Oxford
   University Press

Dahlgreen, J. (2006) Emissions trading in the UK, *Env. L. Rev.* 8(2), 134–43

Defra (2010) *Air Pollution: Action in a Changing Climate*, Department for Environment Food and
   Rural Affairs, Report PB13378, London: TSO

Glossary – Forgotten the meaning of
a word? This quick reference covers
key definitions and other useful terms.

Glossary of terms

The glossary is divided into two parts: *key definitions* and *other useful terms*. The key
definitions can be found within the chapter in which they occur as well as in the glossary
below. These definitions are the essential terms that you must know and understand in
order to prepare for an exam. The additional list of terms provides further definitions of

Guided tour of the companion website

Book resources are available to download. Print your own **topic maps** and **revision checklists!**

Use the **study plan** prior to your revision to help you assess how well you know the subject and determine which areas need most attention. Choose to take the full assessment or focus on targeted study units.

'Test your knowledge' of individual areas with quizzes tailored specifically to each chapter. **Sample problem and essay questions** are also available with guidance on writing a good answer.

Flashcards test and improve recall of important legal terms, key cases and statutes. Available in both electronic and printable formats.

'You be the marker' gives you the chance to evaluate sample exam answers for different question types and understand how and why an examiner awards marks.

Download the **podcast** and listen as your own personal Law Express tutor guides you through answering a typical but challenging question. A step-by-step explanation on how to approach the question is provided, including what essential elements your answer will need for a pass, how to structure a good response, and what to do to make your answer stand out so that you can earn extra marks.

All of this and more can be found when you visit **www.pearsoned.co.uk/lawexpress**

Table of cases and statutes

■ Cases

▮ UK statutes

TABLE OF CASES AND STATUTES

■ Statutory Instruments

◼ Foreign statutes

■ European Union legislation

Decisions

Regulations

Directives

TABLE OF CASES AND STATUTES

Introduction to environmental law

1

■ Topic map

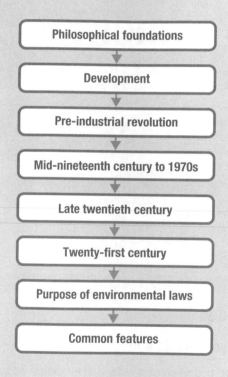

Philosophical foundations

↓

Development

↓

Pre-industrial revolution

↓

Mid-nineteenth century to 1970s

↓

Late twentieth century

↓

Twenty-first century

↓

Purpose of environmental laws

↓

Common features

A printable version of this topic map is available from **www.pearsoned.co.uk/lawexpress**

■ Introduction

Environmental law is often wrongly regarded as being a relatively new and relatively narrow area of law.

Media-friendly topics such as climate change and species extinction lend support to this misconception. In fact, the concepts of environmental law (see Chapter 3 on sources and concepts of environmental law) have developed over decades from loose ideas to much tighter ideas which impact on almost every aspect of twenty-first century life. Hughes *et al.* (2002) expressed the idea neatly, when they said that 'what we had was a number of *diverse laws* relating to the **environment** . . . From these, together with international and European Community law, it has been possible to see the emergence of a more coherent system' (p. 3, italics in original). The New South Wales Environmental Defender's Office (2011) puts it succinctly, saying, 'Environmental law is the area of law that seeks to manage human impacts on the environment' and, though this is a handy label, it is not particularly helpful in trying to understand the boundaries of environmental law, since everything humans do (or don't do!) has an impact on the environment. Bell, McGillivray and Pedersen (2013), furthermore, suggest that there is a 'potential lack of doctrinal certainty' (p. 4) in environmental law, and Pedersen (2013) suggests that 'environmental law represents an incoherent and makeshift body of law' (p. 104). Despite these potential problems, this chapter will explore how environmental law has developed, and why, as well as looking at commonalities and differences.

ASSESSMENT ADVICE

This is a potentially wide topic area and will most likely be assessed using essay questions asking you to analyse underlying themes in the development of environmental law.

Essay questions

Essay questions could be concerned with the temporal shift in the perception of the environment or environmental law. The former has moved from being something which humans needed to be protected from, to that which needs protecting from humans, and the role of the law has changed accordingly.

Other essay questions could relate to the perceived benefits of setting up a specialist environmental court, as has happened elsewhere in the world. ▶

> **Problem questions**
>
> A problem question could be based on interpreting which of a series of scenarios comes under the remit of environmental law, and the rationales for that.
>
> Equally, given the role played in environmental cases by the rule in *Rylands* v *Fletcher* (see below), a problem question based on this is possible.

■ Sample question

Could you answer this question? Below is a typical essay question that could arise on this topic. Guidelines on answering the question are included at the end of this chapter, whilst a sample problem question and guidance on tackling it can be found on the companion website.

ESSAY QUESTION

Assess the impacts on society of the changing role of environmental law since the nineteenth century.

■ The philosophical foundations of environmental law

Coyle and Morrow (2004) state that 'the question of the "philosophical foundation" of environmental thinking in law may strike the lawyer . . . as a strange one' (p. 1) and many would agree. Traditionally humans were viewed separately from the environment, and indeed the philosopher Immanuel Kant (1724–1804) argued that humans have a *right* to exert power over the natural world in a way other species cannot, simply because we have the *ability* to do so. General early attitudes were centred on the subjugation of the natural world by human beings for their benefit, and it was a widely held belief that humans had a right to use 'the environment' as man's larder.

More recent alternatives have centred on the idea that humans are part of the natural world, rather than separate entities, with responsibility to care for it for their own long-term benefit (stewardship), or benefit of other organisms, or both. Professor Lovelock has been a strong proponent of this system of beliefs in the Gaia series of books.

Today, there is still an inevitable conflict between:

- intrinsic/**ecocentric** value (based on simple existence), and
- utilitarian/**anthropocentric** value (based on usefulness to humans).

The ecocentric approach, according to Rowe (1994: 106), is 'grounded in the belief that, compared to the undoubted importance of the human part, the whole ecosphere is even more significant and consequential: more inclusive, more complex, more integrated, more creative, more beautiful, more mysterious, and older than time', whereas an anthropocentric approach simply focuses on 'the human part'.

There has been some rationalisation of these positions by the model of the biosphere as interdependent elements of which humans are a part, and the complexity of this interdependence means one cannot say that any one element is surplus to requirements. In environmental ethics terms, biosphere protection is a concept beyond **sustainable development** (see Chapter 3 on sources and concepts of environmental law), and it has the following legal effects:

- interdependence needs integrated solutions;
- protection extends beyond just the areas which are economically useful;
- problems require transboundary solutions.

As we will see in the remainder of this book, the shift from anthropocentric to ecocentric approaches is not complete, and neither would we want it to be, but it is a shift nonetheless.

Development of environmental law

Working from the premise that there has been centuries-worth of legislation and policy that impact the environment, but that 'environmental law' is a relatively new creature, we can see that there are four 'ages of environmental law' where the approach of law is distinct, even if the start and end point of the 'ages' is less so.

Pre-industrial revolution

Society prior to the industrial and agricultural revolutions was not nearly as urbanised as it is today. The population of London in 1750, for example, was about 700,000 which had risen to just under 2.4 million by 1850 (Demographia, 2001). Since **pollution** becomes increasingly problematic the more concentrated it becomes, the growth in urbanisation and population density during this period led to pollution starting to have an impact on human health.

There were some environmental measures put into place, however, although these were done on a piecemeal basis, with little coherence or enforcement. Brimblecombe (1987) points out that in 1285, for example, King Edward I set up the first **air pollution** commission to combat the state of London's air, which was polluted from the burning of coal (p. 9), and in 1742 Dr Johnson is known to have called London 'a city which abounds with such heaps of filth as a savage would look on with amazement' (Lomborg, 2001: 163).

Up to the point of the industrial revolution, the main route for cases to be brought was through tort. Given the generally reactive nature of tort, this was, from an environmental protection perspective as well as a harm prevention perspective, not a very satisfactory solution, since the damage to the environment or human health would have to occur before action could be taken.

☐ **REVISION NOTE**

The law of tort, which was the only source of remedy for 'environmental' cases, is covered in depth in *Law Express: Tort Law*.

Mid-nineteenth century to 1970s

Again, using the population of London as a yardstick for measuring urbanisation, we can see that, from around 2.4 million in 1850, it grew to 7.4 million in 1971 (with a peak of 8.6 million in 1939) (Demographia, 2001).

Much legislation was introduced during this period that had an impact on the environment, but the most concerted action was taken under the umbrellas of planning (e.g. the Removal of Nuisances and Prevention of Epidemic Diseases Act 1846) and public health (e.g. the Public Health Act 1875), so the emphasis was still on protecting humans, rather than the environment. Among the most well-known are the Alkali Act of 1863 which, despite the 1285 air pollution measures, created the first pollution inspectorate, and the Clean Air Act 1956, which was enacted as a response to the deadly photochemical smogs that had engulfed London in the early 1950s. It created a body (the 'Clean Air Council') to monitor air quality and report back to the Minister.

KEY STATUTE

Clean Air Act 1956

1.(1) Subject to the provisions of this Act, dark smoke shall not be emitted from a chimney of any building, and if, on any day, dark smoke is so emitted, the occupier of the building shall be guilty of an offence.

. . .

23.(1) For the purposes of –

(a) keeping under review the progress made (whether under this Act or otherwise) in abating the pollution of the air in England and Wales; and

(b) obtaining the advice of persons having special knowledge, experience or responsibility in regard to prevention of pollution of the air;

the Minister of Housing and Local Government shall appoint a consultative council, to be called the Clean Air Council, of which he shall be the chairman.

As you can see, the legislation that would now be classed as environmental law was generally still reactive, and focused on particular problems that had been encountered.

 Make your answer stand out

Two articles will be particularly useful to you at this stage of tracing the history of environmental law. Morag-Levine (2011) links precautionary regulation (see Chapter 3 on sources and concepts of environmental law) with Victorian measures, and argues that the reactive approach which is commonly ascribed to this era may need revising. Pontin (2007) contrasts the IPPC regime (see Chapter 6 on environmental permitting) with Victorian measures, and shows 'levels of sophistication in environmental law and policy during the early stages of industrialisation'.

The use of tort is still of great importance in this period and, indeed, was generally the only route which was available for ordinary citizens to try and rectify harm. The available remedies were to change with the case of *Rylands* v *Fletcher*, when Blackburn J set out a new rule (now known as the rule in *Rylands* v *Fletcher*) in the Court of Exchequer (see below). The rule was later confirmed by the House of Lords in *Rylands* v *Fletcher* (1868) LR 3 HL 330, where Cairns LJ referred to a '**non-natural use**' of land (at 339) and has now developed into an accepted part of the legal framework. There was an addition to the rule in the Australian case of *Rickards* v *Lothian* [1913] AC 263 when Moulton LJ said (at 279): 'It is not every use to which land is put that brings into play that principle [*Rylands* v *Fletcher*]. It must be some special use bringing with it increased danger to others, and must not merely be the ordinary use of the land or such a use as is proper for the general benefit of the community.'

KEY CASE

Rylands v *Fletcher* (1865–66) LR 1 Ex 265

Concerning: causes of action; damage; land drainage; mines; negligence; neighbouring land; nuisance

Facts

A reservoir was constructed by a contractor on land. Once filled, the water flooded into mineshafts on neighbouring land. ▶

> **Legal principle**
>
> Subsequently known as the rule in *Rylands* v *Fletcher*, the principle that emerged from this case is that: 'One, who for his own purposes brings upon his land and collects and keeps there anything likely to do mischief if it escapes, must keep it in at his peril, and, if he does not do so, is *prima facie* answerable for all the damage which was the natural consequence of its escape.' (Per Blackburn J at 279)

KEY DEFINITION: 'Non-natural use'

Bingham LJ in *Transco Plc* v *Stockport Metropolitan Borough Council* [2004] 2 AC 1 at 4:

'In determining whether a particular use is to be regarded as ordinary the following factors are relevant:

(i) the extent to which the activity is common, customary or usual (see *Stovin* v *Wise* [1996] AC 923, 949);

(ii) the nature and extent of any foreseeable danger to others created by the carrying out of the activity (see *Cambridge Water Co* v *Eastern Counties Leather plc* [1994] 2 AC 264, 309);

(iii) whether the activity is being carried on for profit or the personal gratification of its author;

(iv) whether the person carrying on the activity is doing so out of the exercise of choice or under compulsion;

(v) the extent, if any, of the social utility of the activity (see *Marcic* v *Thames Water Utilities Ltd* [2002] QB 929'.

The close of the twentieth century

In the 1970s, there was a growing awareness both of the potential knock-on effects on human health of damage to flora and fauna, and larger environmental issues such as nuclear power and the ozone layer, and of the economic impact that this damage could have.

International and EU laws have helped to shape national legislation, and the accession of the UK to the then EEC in 1973, following the European Communities Act 1972, ties in with the start of the First European Environmental Action Programme (OJ C 112, 20 December 1973), which sought to proactively apply the key **polluter pays principle** (see Chapter 3 on sources and concepts of environmental law) to European law. This proactive approach to law-making was adopted in the UK, although one of the earliest pieces of environmental law in this period, the Control of Pollution Act 1974, was a reaction to the fragmented state of existing pollution laws – what Bell, McGillivray and Pedersen (2013) call '[the beginning of] the process of trying to produce a coherent body of environmental law' (p. 24).

KEY CASE

R v HM Inspectorate of Pollution, ex parte Greenpeace (No. 2) [1994] 4 All ER 329; [1994] Env LR 76 (The *Greenpeace* Case)

Concerning: environmental law; judicial review; locus standi; nuclear waste; pressure groups

Facts

Greenpeace sought to challenge HMIP's decision to allow nuclear reprocessing at the THORP plant in Cumbria. Case revolved around whether Greenpeace had sufficient *locus standi* to bring an action in judicial review.

Legal principle

Normally Greenpeace would not have been considered to have had sufficient locus standi, but Otton J said that Greenpeace was 'an entirely responsible and respected body with a genuine concern for the environment' and this led to their bona fide interest in the case. The case is significant as it widened the range of groups which might be able to satisfy the *locus standi* requirements.

This period also saw the passage of the Environmental Protection Act 1990 and the Environment Act 1995 which, between them, set the tone for environmental law in the UK for the next decade or so, with the creation of the Environment Agency (see Chapter 4 on enforcement of environmental law) and the consolidation and codification of existing environmental legislation.

An environmental court for the UK

In 2000, the Department of the Environment, Transport and the Regions (DETR) published the report of the Environmental Court Project, which had been led by Professor Grant. The project looked at the advantages and disadvantages of a specialist court, along the lines of the Land and Environment Court set up in New South Wales in 1979. The advantages and disadvantages of such a court can each be summarised in one statement:

Advantage: Expert lawyers, judges, etc. speed up legal process.

Disadvantage: The 'environmental' aspect of a case may only be one element of it, so the case may need to be split.

 Make your answer stand out

The debate about the usefulness of a specialist environmental court in the UK is a recurring one. For recent discussions see Palmer (2009), who looks at the New Zealand Environment Court, and questions whether it would be 'a welcome introduction in the UK'; Hockman (2009) and Pedersen (2012) who take a different tack and argue for ▶

the introduction of an International Environmental Court; and Gupta (2011) who argued that there is a need for a full review of legislation and judicial structure in India before 'the issue of establishing a specialised environmental court' is decided. Schall (2008), on the other hand, suggests that much of the environmental public interest litigation is already being brought before the European Court of Human Rights.

Twenty-first century environmental law

One of the areas that you might be asked to address is where environmental law is likely to go in the future. Whilst all predictions of the future are fraught with difficulty, looking at the current developments will help to give you a picture of where things might go.

Proactive measures

Governments are starting to look at environmental issues in a *strategic* manner, and increasingly legislation is being introduced with the aim of preventing potential environmental harm by setting standards and using preventative procedures. The Integrated Pollution Prevention and Control regime (IPPC, or Environmental Permitting in the UK) is a good example of this, and is discussed later (in Chapter 6 on environmental permitting).

Wider scale

The twenty-first century has also seen a growth in recognition that environmental issues are not necessarily just of national concern. The obvious examples of this are climate change and the transboundary nature of pollution.

In the 1970s it was recognised that industrial pollution from the UK was causing acid rain which was damaging forests and fisheries in Scandinavia (RCEP, 1976), and this was followed by the low-level radioactive contamination of sheep in north Wales following the accident at the Chernobyl reactor in the Ukraine in 1986.

There has also been a recognition that developing countries are going to need assistance from the developed world if they are to fulfil their potential in a manner which preserves resources.

Embodiment of theoretical concepts as principles of law

Environmental law-making in the twenty-first century has seen a growth in the use of basic theoretical ideas such as sustainability and biodiversity in legislation. Indeed, sustainability (see Chapter 3 on sources and concepts of environmental law for more details) did not feature greatly in name (though in reality did in nature) before the UN Conference on Environment and Development in 1992. It is now embedded in legislation (e.g. the Sustainable Communities Act 2007), although McEldowney and McEldowney (2010) point out that it is 'likely to be interpreted and acted upon differently at each level of government' (p. 46).

Public participation

With the Åarhus Convention (on Access to Information, Public Participation in Decision-making and Access to Justice in Environmental Matters) coming into force in 2001, the role of public participation in environmental law-making has increased dramatically. The Convention built on a body of legislation and case law that has gradually emerged from Directive 90/313/EEC on the freedom of access to information on the environment (and Directive 2003/4/EC on public access to environmental information, which repealed it), the *Greenpeace* case in 1994, via the Human Rights Act 1998 and Freedom of Information Act 2000, and the current regime of public involvement is unprecedented, although Lee and Abbot (2003) question how far it works in practice.

■ The purpose of environmental law

There are two possibilities of purpose for environmental law. First, and this was definitely the case in the early stages of the process, the law exists to protect people. Cleaning up the air, the sea and rivers were all done under the banner of improving public health, and often (though not always) there were benefits for the wider environment as well.

If the two purposes are viewed as hands on a clock face, environmental law is at its most effective when both hands point to the same point on the clock – in other words, when the legislation protects the interests of both humans and the wider environment. By contrast, it is at its least effective when the two hands point in opposite directions.

! Don't be tempted to . . .

A common mistake would be to assume that all environmental laws have the same purpose. There could be a broad range of anthropocentric (human-centred) reasons why the law was introduced – human health, aesthetic, cultural, resource management and so on. An assumption of a single purpose is no more accurate for environmental law than it is for any other type of law, so remember to make sure of the purpose of the specific piece of legislation about which you are writing.

■ Features common to environmental laws

Having seen that there is a body of law that has gradually emerged, and can now be called environmental law, we can still see that there is no single 'law' (this is exacerbated when looking at what 'the environment' might be – see Chapter 2 on definitions of environmental law).

Generally, however, environmental laws seek to control the relationship between humans and the natural environment. They can be:

- Positive in nature: These impose a requirement on a certain course of action, which may be a general duty. For example, Regulation 46(1) of the Environmental Permitting (England and Wales) Regulations 2010 (the Permitting Regulations) includes the words 'the regulator must maintain a register . . .'.

- Negative in nature: These forbid those covered from doing certain acts. For example, Regulation 12 of the Permitting Regulations begins, 'A person must not . . .'.

- Hybrid in nature: Some provisions can be interpreted either way. For example, s. 1(1) of the Nuclear Installations Act 1965, says that no one can use a site for installing or operating a nuclear reactor unless they have been granted a licence. This could be positive ('you must have a licence') or negative ('you must not install a nuclear reactor').

There is also a distinction that can be made between reactive and proactive laws, and this includes several of the examples discussed above. For an environmental law to be proactive in nature, it will generally be an attempt to prevent harm occurring, whereas a reactive environmental law will have to wait for the harm to occur, and then govern the course of action for remeding the damage.

One fundamental issue of environmental law is that in order to work effectively it will need the involvement and cooperation of a range of disciplines – particularly those in the fields of physical and environmental sciences. These disciplines can assist with legislating the constantly changing global environment, as well as predicting the future impacts of actions.

Other disciplines can also help with understanding whether the effects of a certain course of action are likely to be cumulative (that is, there will be no measurable impact for some time), irreversible (species extinction is the best example of this), or both. It is important to know this, as cumulative events generally need quick action, and irreversible ones need careful planning. There is an inherent conflict between these, and between action and the lengthy process of law-making.

✎ EXAM TIP

There is often talk of measures being introduced without proper understanding of their consequences. The landfill tax, for example, is regularly linked to an increase in illegal fly-tipping. Look at the arguments put forward by Pocklington and Pocklington (1998) in the early days of the tax and, more recently, Bennett (2010).

■ Putting it all together

Answer guidelines

See the essay question at the start of the chapter.

Approaching the question

This question is quite broad, but is clearly about both the nature of environmental law, and its scope. It also requires you to think in wider terms about what environmental law is *for* – protection of human health or of the environment.

Important points to include

- You would need to start by defining the terms as you intend to address them. For example, what do you understand by 'impacts on society' or 'environmental law'? Once you have set this out, you can look at the role played by environmental law in the relevant time period.

- As it is a broad topic, you would be able to narrow down the scope of your answer, and focus perhaps on one or two areas that fall within the wider environmental law – waste management and water pollution, for example.

- Assuming you have chosen these areas, then you should move on to outlining the early legislation, and that the focus was on public health, rather than the wider environment. This would allow you to link to 'impacts on society' well – the elimination of cholera in the late nineteenth century, the rise in quality of life and life expectancy and so on.

- As you move to the twentieth and twenty-first centuries, you will be able to assess the way in which environmental law has changed – becoming wider in scope, more proactive in nature and so on, and then look at the impact that this has had on society.

- To finish off, look back over your answer and see whether any themes have emerged – if yes, say so.

 Make your answer stand out

You will be able to look at the role that environmental law has played relatively easily. More contentious is the debate about the role that environmental law should play. Read Kimbrell (2008), Richardson and Wood (eds) (2006) and Bodansky (2009).

READ TO IMPRESS

Bell, S., McGillivray, D. and Pedersen, O. (2013) *Environmental Law*, 8th Edn. Oxford: Oxford University Press

Bennett, O. (2010) Fly-tipping, the illegal dumping of waste, House of Commons Briefing Paper SNSC-05672, London: House of Commons Library

Brimblecombe, P. (1987) *The Big Smoke: History of Air Pollution in London Since Mediaeval Times*, London: Routledge

Bodansky, D. (2009) *The Art and Craft of International Environmental Law*, Harvard: Harvard University Press

Coyle, S. and Morrow, K. (2004) *The Philosophical Foundations of Environmental Law*, Oxford: Hart

Demographia (2001) http://www.demographia.com/db-lonuza1680.htm

Hockman, S. (2009) An international court for the environment, *Env L Rev.* 11(1), 1–4

Hughes, D., Jewell, T., Lowther, J., Parpworth, N. and de Prez, P. (2002) *Environmental Law*, 4th Edn. Oxford: Oxford University Press

Gupta, K. S. (2011) The role of judiciary in promoting sustainable development: need of specialized environment court in India, *Journal of Sustainable Development*, 2011, 4(2), 249–253, doi:10.5539/jsd.v4n2p249

Kimbrell, A. (2008) [Case comment] Halting the global meltdown: can environmental law play a role? *E.L.M.* 20(2), 64–70.

Lee, M. and Abbot, C. (2003) The usual suspects? Public participation under the Åarhus convention, *The Modern Law Review* 66(1), 80–108

Lomborg, B. (2001) *The Sceptical Environmentalist*, Cambridge: Cambridge University Press

McEldowney, P. and McEldowney, S. (2010) *Environmental Law*, Harlow: Longman

Morag-Levine, N. (2011) Is precautionary regulation a civil law instrument? Lessons from the history of the Alkali Act, *J. Env. L.* 23(1), 1–43

The New South Wales Environmental Defender's Office (2011) http://www.edonsw.org.au/introduction_to_environmental_law

Palmer, K. (2009) The environment court in New Zealand: UK application? *E.L.M.* 21(5), 241–9

Pedersen, O. W. (2012) An international environmental court and international legalism, *J. Env. L.* 24(3), 547–558

Pedersen, O. W. (2013) Modest pragmatic lessons for a diverse and incoherent environmental law, *Oxford Journal of Legal Studies*, 33(1), 103–131, doi:10.1093/ojls/gqs026

Pocklington, R. E. and Pocklington, D. N. (1998) The United Kingdom landfill tax – externalities and external influences, *J.P.L.* Jun, 529–45

Pontin, B. (2007) Integrated pollution control in Victorian Britain: rethinking progress within the history of environmental law, *J. Env. L.* 19(2), 173–99

RCEP (1976) *Nuclear Power and the Environment*, Royal Commission on Environmental Pollution, 6th Report, London: HMSO

Richardson, B. and Wood, S. (eds) (2006) *Environmental Law for Sustainability: A Reader*, Oxford: Hart

Rowe, S. (1994) Ecocentrism: the chord that harmonizes humans and earth, *The Trumpeter* 11(2), 106–107

Schall, C. (2008) Public interest litigation concerning environmental matters before human rights courts: a promising future concept?, *J. Env. L.* 20(3), 417–53

www.pearsoned.co.uk/lawexpress

Go online to access more revision support including quizzes to test your knowledge, sample questions with answer guidelines, podcasts you can download, and more!

Definitions of environmental law

2

Revision checklist

Essential points you should know:

☐ What environmental law is

☐ How to define key terms in environmental law (e.g. the environment, waste, pollution)

☐ The need for unified definitions

☐ The impact of environmental law on quality of life, e.g. by controlling climate change, planning, drinking water

Topic map

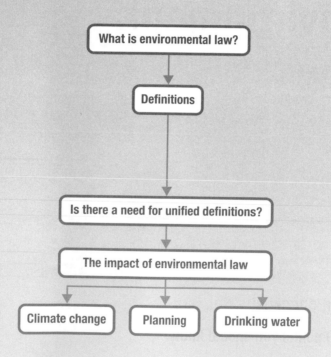

■ Introduction

Since the environment (and thus environmental law) is such a wide field (or possibly not even a coherent subject), there are inherent difficulties in trying to be too prescriptive as to what is, and is not, 'environmental law'.

There is a general purpose to environmental law, and there are some features that are common to many different aspects of environmental law, but there is no single entity that can be described accurately as 'environmental law'.

ASSESSMENT ADVICE

This topic area could be equally assessed using either problem questions asking you to apply definitions to particular situations or essay questions asking you to analyse underlying themes in the development of environmental law. Whichever method is used, the similarity is that they will be concerned with the temporal shift in the perception of 'the environment' (from dangerous wilderness, through rich resource, to fragile system), 'pollution' or 'waste'.

There is not a great deal of case law in this area of the topic, but what case law there is will hinge around interpretations of some of the key terms.

Essay questions

Obvious essay questions are:

- Assess the extent to which environmental law needs a single definition in order to operate effectively.
- Analyse the extent to which environmental law has played a role in shaping society.

Problem questions

Problem questions could relate to the definitional aspects of environmental law alone, or could be presented in combination with some of the more substantive topic areas.

◼ Sample question

Could you answer this question? Below is a typical problem question that could arise on this topic. Guidelines on answering the question are included at the end of this chapter, whilst a sample essay question and guidance on tackling it can be found on the companion website.

PROBLEM QUESTION

John owns an industrial site and, in 2001, he received a large quantity of leftover stone, which was a by-product of nearby stone quarrying work. He has stored this leftover stone on his site and, although he has no specific plans for it, thinks it may well have possible uses at some point in the future.

John has now been informed that this leftover stone counts as 'waste' under the Waste Framework Directive.

Advise John as to whether or not this is the case.

◼ Definitions of environment, waste and pollution

These terms are all used in everyday life, and each has several meanings, ranging from the general and commonplace to the very specific and specialist. At a day-to-day level, a measure of uncertainty around meaning is hardly a problem, as most of the general definitions have a number of marked similarities. However, from a legal, statutory interpretation perspective, the lack of an agreed definition could pose significant problems, and could ultimately determine the success or otherwise of legal action.

✎ EXAM TIP

When discussing definitions in your answer, particularly if it is as part of a broader question, be clear about which definition you will be applying, and why it is the most appropriate.

The environment

The current statutory definition of the environment as far as the UK is concerned is found in the Environmental Protection Act 1990 (EPA) but, inevitably, this definition only applies to the extent that the statute itself does. From an EU perspective, even though the EU Sustainable Development Strategy 'added a third, environmental dimension to the Lisbon Strategy of economic and social renewal' (DG Environment, 2012), there is no single definition of the environment – indeed many directives seem to deliberately avoid such a definition (see Art. 2 of Directive 2008/1/EC concerning integrated pollution prevention and control, for example). Two of the definitions are presented below and, given the relationship between EU law and UK statute, all three of these definitions could apply in the UK.

KEY DEFINITION: The environment

Section 1(2) Environmental Protection Act 1990:

'The Environment' consists of all, or any of the following media, namely the air, water and land, and the medium of air includes the air within buildings and within other natural or manmade structures above or below ground.

Directive 79/831/EEC (on the approximation of the laws, regulations and administrative provisions relating to the classification, packaging and labelling of dangerous substances):

'Environment' means water, air and land and their interrelationship as well as relationships between them and any living organisms.

First Environmental Action Programme, 1973:

'Environment' means the combination of elements whose complex interrelationships make up the setting, the surroundings and the conditions of life of the individual and of society as they are and as they are felt.

Bulgarian Environmental Protection Act 1991 (Additional Provisions, §1(1)):

'Environment' means a complex of natural and anthropogenic factors and elements that are mutually interrelated and affect the ecological equilibrium and the quality of life, human health, the cultural and historical heritage and the landscape.

It is clear to see that as these definitions move farther back in time, the broader and more ethereal the definition becomes. It is also important to keep in mind the purpose of these three definitions – the First Environmental Action Programme was a four-year programme designed to shape future environmental policies within the then EEC, so can afford to be a little broad, whereas the EPA is, *inter alia*, designed to impose statutory rights and duties, and thus must be comparatively prescriptive.

The exception is the Bulgarian EPA, which is the most recent of the definitions, and is expressed in what appear to be largely subjective terms. Since Bulgaria has been an EU member state since 2007, one would expect to see an alignment between the four definitions above but, in practice, this is limited.

What are the key elements of a definition of the environment?

All of these are present in the definitions above and, depending on the purpose of the definition, all are equally applicable:

- different media: air, water, land;
- interaction/interrelationship between them;
- living organisms (including humans);
- the built environment.

✎ EXAM TIP

An essay question on the lack of a single definition for 'the environment' could be tackled by means of a comparison of definitions, as well as an analysis of their interrelationship and purpose, and this would allow you to explore fundamental issues such as the role of soft and hard international law (see Chapter 3 on sources and concepts of environmental law) in shaping definitions.

Waste

There will be a great deal more coverage of waste management in Chapter 9 on waste management, but at this stage it is worth investigating what waste actually might be.

From an EU perspective, the source of waste legislation was the 1975 Waste Framework Directive (Directive 75/442/EEC), and this was supplemented by various other provisions, before being codified by Directive 2006/12/EC on waste and amended by Directive 2998/09/EC.

KEY DEFINITION: Waste

Section 75(2) Environmental Protection Act 1990 (as enacted):

'Waste' includes –

(a) any substance which constitutes a scrap material or an effluent or other unwanted surplus substance arising from the application of any process; and

(b) any substance or article which requires to be disposed of as being broken, worn out, contaminated or otherwise spoiled.

. . .

Section 75(2) Environmental Protection Act 1990 (as amended by Para. 88(2) Sch. 2 Environment Act 1995):

'Waste' means any substance or object in the categories set out in Schedule 2B to this Act which the holder discards or intends or is required to discard . . .

Article 3(1) Directive 2008/98/EC on waste:

'Waste' shall mean any substance or object which the holder discards or intends or is required to discard.

(This was the same in Directive 75/442/EEC, Directive 91/156/EEC and Directive 2006/12/EC.)

Article 2, 1989 Basel Convention (on the Control of Transboundary Movements of Hazardous Wastes and their Disposal):

'Wastes' are substances or objects which are disposed of or are intended to be disposed of or are required to be disposed of by the provisions of national law.

As can be seen from the definitions above, there is currently a measure of concurrence as to the statutory definition of waste.

The UK, however, had a different definition of waste until the Environment Act 1995 brought the statute more into line with regional and international provisions.

The current definitions all have as their core the requirement that the matter which is classed as waste is, or will be, discarded.

However, under the now defunct landfill tax scheme (introduced by the Finance Act 1996), a slightly different approach to waste was used, since the aim was to promote recycling and reduce landfilled waste. The case of *Parkwood Landfill* (below) explores this idea further, and shows how the same item could be classed as 'waste' and 'not waste' at the same time.

KEY CASE

Customs and Excise Commissioners v Parkwood Landfill Ltd [2002] EWCA Civ 1707

Concerning: landfill tax; recycling; waste materials

Facts

Sheffield City Council disposed of unwanted materials from highway works, for a fee, to a recycling plant operated by R. R subsequently divided the unwanted material into that which was recyclable and saleable. The latter was sold to P which used it for road making and landscaping purposes at its landfill site. Customs maintained that P was liable to landfill tax in respect of the saleable materials, but P argued that the materials were no longer waste when deposited at its premises.

Legal principle

Material deposited at a landfill site but subsequently recycled and reused was not 'waste' for landfill tax purposes (although it would still be waste as far as the Waste Framework was concerned).

Pollution

If obtaining accurate definitions for 'the environment' and 'waste' is important then equally, if not more, of a challenge is an accurate definition of pollution. McEldowney and McEldowney (2010) say that 'another way to describe Environmental Law is to concentrate on the harm caused to the environment by human activity' (p. 7) and, indeed, Chapter 1 showed that one element of the role of environmental law is to protect the environment from pollution, so knowing what constitutes each is essential. However, as Wolf and Stanley (2010) point out, 'there is no single, accepted, definition of pollution' (p. 3). Below are three different definitions that have been used and, in any essay or problem question based on what pollution might be, it is important to remember this range of possibilities.

KEY DEFINITION: Pollution

RCEP, 1972, Pollution in Some British Estuaries and Coastal Waters, 3rd Report of the Royal Commission on Environmental Pollution, Cmnd 5054:

'Pollution' is the introduction by man into the environment of substances or energy liable to cause hazards to human health, harm to living resources and ecological systems, damage to structure or amenity or interference with legitimate uses of the environment.

Section 1(3) Environmental Protection Act 1990 'Pollution of the Environment means . . .':

pollution of the environment due to the release (into any environmental medium) from any process of substances which are capable of causing harm to man or any other living organisms supported by the environment.

Bulgarian Environmental Protection Act 1991 (Additional Provisions, §1(5)):

'pollution of the environment' means the change of its qualities as a result of the occurrence and introduction of physical, chemical or biological factors from a natural or anthropogenic source.

Oxford Concise Dictionary of Ecology:

The defilement of the natural environment by a by-product of human activities which enters or becomes concentrated in the environment, where it may cause injury to humans.

There is a contrast here between the RCEP and Oxford dictionary definitions, which require that the 'polluting thing' be introduced by man, and the statutory definitions from the UK and Bulgaria which include, explicitly or implicitly, naturally occurring pollution (for example, the methane produced in a mangrove swamp).

By contrast, s. 85 of the Water Resources Act 1991 (WRA), and subsequently Reg. 12 of the Environmental Permitting (England and Wales) Regulations 2010 chose not to define pollution at all, relying instead on creating offences of causing or knowingly permitting 'any poisonous, noxious or polluting matter or any solid waste matter to enter any controlled waters' (s. 85(1) WRA) and causing or knowingly permitting a '**water discharge activity**' (Reg. 12(b)).

Both the RCEP and statutory definitions are factored on the potential of material to cause harm ('liable to' and 'capable of'), rather than it actually causing harm. This ties in with the WRA approach, confirmed in *R* v *Dovermoss* [1995] Env LR 258, 265 in which 'It is not necessary . . . to establish actual harm' to find pollution, but 'the likelihood or capability of causing harm . . . is sufficient.' Water pollution is covered in greater depth in Chapter 8 on water pollution.

❗ Don't be tempted to . . .

Don't be tempted to rush into a question about definitions without looking at the application of them in relation to the question. Consider, for example:

- What is the definition that is most relevant to the facts?
- What exactly is the question asking you to do?
- Is there an option of considering the merits of different definitions?

It is clear then, that a topic dealing with potential pollution of the environment by the misplacement of waste is going to be hampered to a greater or lesser extent by the different ways in which the three key terms can be interpreted. For practical purposes, however, the remainder of this text will work on the statutory definition unless expressly stated otherwise.

Is there a need for unified definitions?

With a myriad of different definitions for all of these categories, it would be easy to jump to the conclusion in an essay that having a single definition for each of 'the environment', 'waste' and 'pollution' would lead to a simpler, better system of regulation. This would be folly, however, as the fundamental question about all definitions is the extent to which they are fit for purpose.

The literature seems generally to be moving towards single definitions for very specific aspects of, for example, waste. The List of Wastes (England) Regulations 2005, for example, gives effect to the European List of Wastes (formerly European Waste Catalogue), and classifies different types of waste by a six-digit code (see Chapter 9 on waste management).

There appear to be no drives towards single, general definitions, and your answers should reflect this.

■ How environmental law affects quality of life

Taking the definitions of 'the environment', 'waste' and 'pollution' outlined above, and the developments covered in Chapter 1, we can see that 'environmental law' in its plethora of forms impacts upon the quality of life (both human and non-human) in many different ways.

Climate change

In 1988, the United Nations General Assembly passed Resolution 43/53, which, *inter alia*, 'Recognizes that climate change is a common concern of mankind, since climate is an essential condition which sustains life on earth' (UNGA A/Res/43/53 Protection of global climate for present and future generations of mankind) and, as such, the impact that environmental law has had on climate change (and vice versa) is fundamental.

> ✎ **EXAM TIP**
>
> There is now general scientific consensus concerning the links between anthropogenic CO_2 production (that caused by humans) and climate change, but being aware of some of the counter-arguments put forward by some scientists and lawyers will make your answer more balanced.

Specifics concerning legislation in this area will be covered in Chapter 7 on air pollution, but clearly the links between environmental law and the quality of life in this instance are irrefutable.

Make your answer stand out

If you are asked to assess the impact of environmental law on climate change regime, consider looking at the question from a national, EU and international perspective, as this might make a difference to your answer. Nationally, for example, measures such as the Climate Change Act 2008 (see Chapter 7 on air pollution) have introduced things like targets and carbon budgets, and much of this approach has been distilled from EU and international law. On the wider scale, however, there are debates about the fairness and efficacy of such targets and budgets in the developed world, when China and India remain effectively unregulated (see Vinuales, 2011; Vanderheiden, 2008).

Planning

Discussed in more detail in Chapter 5, planning law essentially governs the use of space and the impact of **development** on the environment. As such, it is a physical manifestation of such principles of international environmental law as the precautionary principle, sustainable development and biodiversity. On a more local scale, through environmental impact assessments or the environmental permitting regime (see Chapter 6 on environmental permitting), planning law can have an impact on quality of life by ensuring that polluting industries and residential areas are kept separate (see, for example, *Lopéz Ostra* v *Spain* (1994) 20 EHRR 277, or *Öneryildiz* v *Turkey* [2004] ECHR 657).

Drinking water

One of the basic requirements of human life is water that is safe to drink. Chapter 8 on water pollution looks at the details of the law relating to water pollution, but it is clear that environmental law has been one of the mechanisms through which policies for improving the quality of drinking water have been implemented. The links between clean drinking water and health have been understood since the mid-nineteenth century, when the 1854 cholera outbreak in Soho was traced to a contaminated pump in Broad Street. The Metropolis Water Act 1852 had already led to the building of some new sewerage infrastructure in London by this time, following previous cholera outbreaks, but the Soho outbreak expedited their completion.

■ Putting it all together

Answer guidelines

See the problem question at the start of the chapter.

Approaching the question

This question is clearly about definitions of waste and, with no indication to the contrary, can be taken to be based in England. It asks you to address your answer to a specific perspective, that of advising John, and so, at the very least, you should do that.

Important points to include

- Start by addressing the issues – this is inert material, and so the question is not asking about hazardous waste.
- Secondly, you should outline the definition of waste found in the Waste Framework Directive (which is the basis for that in the EPA as amended) and then applied to the facts of the case.

▶

- Clearly this question has links to the old *Parkwood* case discussed above, and so a good answer would deal with the points raised in that case. There are also similarities with the more recent case of *Environment Agency* v *Inglenorth Ltd* [2009] EWHC 670 (Admin).

 Make your answer stand out

The definition of 'waste' has been problematic for many years and you might like to address the debate about whether having such a potentially broad definition is a sensible approach to the topic.

Previous European case law could be traced – for example, the scenario is based entirely on Case C-9/00 *Palin Granit Oy and Vehmassalon kansanterveystyon kuntayhtymän hallitus*, which held that: 'the holder of leftover stone resulting from stone quarrying which was stored for an indefinite length of time to await possible use discarded or intended to discard that leftover stone. It was accordingly to be classified as waste within the meaning of Council Directive 75/442/EEC of 15 July 1975 on waste.'

READ TO IMPRESS

Bell, S., McGillivray, D. and Pedersen, O. (2013) *Environmental Law*, 8th Edn. Oxford: Oxford University Press

DG Environment (2012) *Sustainable Development*, European Commission Directorate-General Environment

McEldowney, P. and McEldowney, S. (2010) *Environmental Law*, Harlow: Longman

Vanderheiden, S. (ed.) (2008) *Political Theory and Climate Change*, Boston: MIT Press

Vinuales, J. E. (2011) Balancing effectiveness and fairness in the redesign of the climate change regime, *L.J.I.L.* 24(1), 223–52

Wolf, S. and Stanley, N. (2010) *Wolf and Stanley on Environmental Law*, 5th Edn. London: Routledge

www.pearsoned.co.uk/lawexpress

 Go online to access more revision support including quizzes to test your knowledge, sample questions with answer guidelines, podcasts you can download, and more!

Sources and concepts of environmental law

3

Revision checklist

Essential points you should know:

☐ The main sources of environmental law (e.g. international, EU, common law and legislation)

☐ The key concepts and principles of environmental law (e.g. sustainable development, the precautionary principle, the polluter pays principle)

☐ Possible emergent concepts and principles of environmental law (e.g. a human right to a safe and healthy environment)

■ Topic map

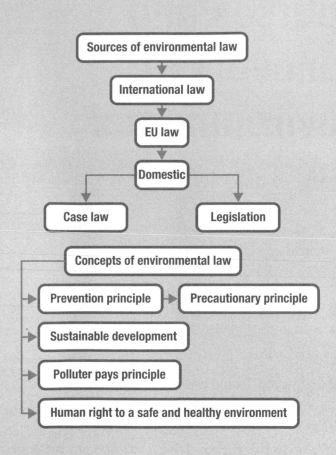

A printable version of this topic map is available from **www.pearsoned.co.uk/lawexpress**

■ Introduction

Knowing where environmental law started, what it could be and should be, is only the start. You also need to be able to answer questions on where environmental law comes from – not in an historic sense, but in a modern-day sense.

The discussions about the relationship between international law, EU law and domestic law are going to be specific to environmental law, and for a more detailed revision guide to EU law you should refer to Ewan Kirk's *Law Express: EU Law* 2012. Textbooks such as Birnie, Boyle and Redgewell (2009) are also useful to give a much more detailed international law perspective on the environment.

The second part of the chapter will allow you to recap the guiding concepts that have emerged from international and EU law and shape all current environmental law and policy. Phrases such as 'sustainable development' and 'the polluter pays' are used by politicians, educators and the media on an almost daily basis, but what do they actually mean from a legal perspective, and where do they come from? As Castro (2004) states, 'mainstream analyses of this concept and its significance differ enormously from those of critical approaches', so perhaps the (grammatically questionable) question might be, 'What *are* sustainable development?'

The chapter finishes with a look at concepts of environmental law that might be developing, and could well become mainstream in the forthcoming years.

ASSESSMENT ADVICE

Assessments here could look at the relationship between the different sources of law, and the incorporation of general concepts into enforceable principles of law. Make sure that you understand the hierarchy of laws both in terms of the relationship between international, EU and domestic law, and the relationship between the various courts that may be involved. Remember that the creation of the Supreme Court in October 2009 replaced the House of Lords.

■ Sample question

Could you answer this question? Below is a typical essay question that could arise on this topic. Guidelines on answering the question are included at the end of this chapter, whilst a sample problem question and guidance on tackling it can be found on the companion website.

ESSAY QUESTION

Assess the extent to which it is true to say that the source(s) of environmental law affect its impact.

International law

There are many ideas about what international law might be – as Cassese (2004) says: 'the first salient feature of international law is that most of its rules aim at regulating the behaviour of States, not that of individuals' (p. 3).

Where does that leave international *environmental* law then? Vinuales (2011) argues that international environmental law (IEL) has existed since the 1960s, but has been struggling with legitimacy, effectiveness and fairness (p. 223). On the other hand, the Permanent Court of Arbitration, in The Hague, which has no problems with legitimacy, effectiveness or fairness, suggests that IEL has its roots in the United Nations Conference on the Human Environment in 1972 (PCA/CPA, 2005 'Iron Rhine Arbitration' Para. 59).

For the purposes of this text, however, the roots of IEL are less important than the effect it has on other laws, be they EU or domestic. Bell, McGillivray and Pedersen (2013: 138) argue that IEL is important as some environmental issues are of such a scale that only international action will be able to tackle them.

International law, environmental or otherwise, tends to be separated into 'hard' law and 'soft' law. 'There is considerable debate as to what, within the field of Environmental Law, constitutes "rules" or "principles"; what is "soft law"; and which environmental treaty law or principles have contributed to the development of customary international law' (PCA/CPA, 2005 'Iron Rhine Arbitration' Para. 58).

Hard law

Hard law is generally the term given to international law that is, in some way, binding. It can be divided into treaties, case law and custom and juristic works.

Treaties

Treaties in international law are not always called 'Treaty' – they can also go by the name Convention, Protocol (to a Convention), Covenant, Pact, Act and so on. To make matters more complicated, some are very specific, and contain high levels of detail, whereas others are Framework or Umbrella agreements, where the detail is left to later instruments. The best-known example of a Framework agreement is the United Nations Framework Convention on Climate Change (FCCC), which was opened for signature in May 1992, after the UNCED Conference in Rio de Janeiro. The FCCC set no emissions targets itself, and it was left to subsequent measures (notably the 1997 Kyoto Protocol) to put in place binding targets.

Depending on the type of government, states will usually have to ratify the signature of the Head of State (for example) by approval of their respective parliaments. This is the case in the UK since, per Oliver LJ in *Maclaine Watson & Co Ltd* v *DTI* [1989] 3 All ER 523, 'a treaty is not part of English law unless and until it has been incorporated into the law by legislation' (p. 545).

Often treaties will only come into effect if a certain number of signatories ratify – this can be expressed as a hard number (e.g. the FCCC, which would 'enter into force on the ninetieth day after the date of deposit of the fiftieth instrument of **ratification**' (Art. 23)) or as a more complicated formula (e.g. the Kyoto Protocol, which would 'enter into force on the ninetieth day after the date on which not less than 55 Parties to the Convention, incorporating Parties included in Annex I which accounted in total for at least 55 per cent of the total carbon dioxide emissions for 1990 of the Parties included in Annex I, have deposited their instruments of ratification, acceptance, approval or accession' (Art. 25(1))). Treaties are generally only binding on those states which have ratified them.

! Don't be tempted to . . .

When looking at a convention, treaty or other instrument of hard law, remember to ensure that (a) the UK has signed/ratified it, and (b) that it has come into force. The New York Convention on the Law of the Non-Navigational Uses of International Watercourses, for example, was signed in 1997, but is not yet in force.

Case law

There are only two permanent international judicial tribunals, and these are the International Court of Justice (ICJ) and the International Criminal Court (ICC), both of which sit in The Hague. Very occasionally environmental cases come before the ICJ (for example, Whaling in the Antarctic (*Australia* v *Japan* (2010)) but, to date, no environmental case has been heard by the ICC and, indeed, it is unlikely that one will ever fall within its remit.

Unlike English law, which has a well-established doctrine of binding precedent (see Finch and Fafinski, *Law Express: English Legal System,* 2012), the ICJ gives many decisions and opinions, and uses past decisions to assist it (although the precedent is not binding).

In addition to the permanent courts, there may be informal systems put in place by many of the treaties to adjudicate in case of disputes. Article XVIII(1) of the 1973 Convention on International Trade in Endangered Species of Wild Fauna and Flora (CITES) for example, states that:

Any dispute which may arise between two or more Parties with respect to the interpretation or application of the provisions of the present Convention shall be subject to negotiation between the Parties involved in the dispute.

Although not a formal court, the Permanent Court of Arbitration (PCA) at The Hague, mentioned above, 'provides services for the resolution of disputes involving various combinations of states, state entities, intergovernmental organizations, and private parties' (PCA, 2011). Returning to CITES, Article XVIII(2) states that states can refer issues to the PCA 'and the Parties submitting the dispute shall be bound by the arbitral decision'.

Custom and juristic works

New concepts are often not introduced through treaties but through customs generally accepted by states. The unanswerable question here is, of course, the issue of exactly when custom becomes part of international law. Writings by respected commentators are often referred to by courts and arbitrators when settling disputes, including on whether a particular custom has become law.

Soft law

Soft law, which is 'not binding in form, is often neither clear nor specific in content, and is not readily enforceable in character' (Bell, McGillivray and Pedersen, 2013: 147), can sometimes be seen as the 'means' to the hard law 'end' – as Barczewski suggests, 'soft law instruments can be intentionally used to generate support for or to help generate binding hard law' (2011: 54). Soft law is generally broken down into declarations, principles, and recommendations.

Declarations and principles

More of a non-binding 'declaration of intent' by states than a binding promise to do something. The most significant environmental examples came out of the UNCHE in Stockholm in 1973, the UNCED in Rio de Janeiro in 1992 and, some would argue, the World Summit on Sustainable Development in Johannesburg in 2002. Bell, McGillivray and Pedersen (2013: 147) outline the functions of these declarations thus:

> They consolidate and restate what are already rules of customary international law . . . they contribute towards moving principles forward to the status of custom; and they reflect the agreed aspirations of the international community.

It is this aspirational quality that marks out declarations from binding law, as states may be reluctant to sign up to a range of binding targets in a particular area, being happier to agree to a broader signalling of intentions.

Recommendations

Recommendations such as those found in UN or OECD publications can form the basis for policy both internationally and nationally. Recommendations may become principles, and these may in turn develop into declaration and hard law, but this is not guaranteed.

Make your answer stand out

There is a fascinating and on-going debate about whether soft international law is a useful element of law. Blutman (2010) argues that 'soft law' does not have a 'coherent and persuasive foundation' (p. 605) and that this means that it 'cannot be defended in the context of international law' (p. 606). Kaufmann-Kohler (2010), on the other hand, argues that 'soft law carries a certain normative weight' (p. 299) and that criticism of it 'is undoubtedly excessive, but cannot be discarded completely' (p. 298). This is to some extent backed up by Ellis (2012). A third view is put forward by Barelli (2009) who states that 'soft law cannot be simply dismissed as non-law' (p. 959). You could show your awareness of this debate by incorporating it into an answer about hard and soft international law, and commenting on it.

EU law

As an environmental law revision guide, the coverage of EU law here is intended as a broad outline only. Specific pieces of legislation and case law will be covered in the chapter of this text which deals with that particular topic. For more detail on the wider implications of EU law, please refer to Ewan Kirk's *Law Express: EU Law* (2012). Generally, EU law can be divided into:

- Primary legislation (treaties of the European Union and regulations): broadly speaking, these need no national legislation to give them effect, as they are directly applicable (see Kirk, 2012 for further explanation).

- Secondary legislation (directives and decisions): these will need the member state(s) to introduce legislation dealing with, and implementing, the subject matter.

As with international law, there are also non-binding recommendations and opinions.

! Don't be tempted to . . .

When looking at environmental legislation, don't confuse regulations made by the EU, which are primary legislation, and regulations made as secondary legislation in the UK.

Initially set up as the European *Economic* Community, the EEC did not consider that the environment was within its competency, as it had been set up as a primarily economic entity. The UNCHE in Stockholm in 1972 was followed the same year by the Paris Summit meeting of the (then six) EEC member states where they declared:

Economic expansion is not an end in itself . . . it should result in an improvement in the quality of life as well as standards of living. As befits the genius of Europe, particular attention will be given to intangible values and to protecting the environment, so that progress may really be put at the service of mankind (Declaration of the Council of the European Communities and of the representatives of the Governments of the Member States meeting in the Council of 22 November 1973 on the programme of action of the European Communities on the environment, OJ C 112, 20.12.1973, p. 1).

This declaration led directly to the first of six European environmental action programmes (EAPs). The first five of these were simply outline political statements on legislation, but the sixth EAP has been adopted in the form of a legally binding decision.

European environmental action programmes (EAPs)

The ideas put forward in the first EAP, which ran from 1973 to 1977, marked a radical change from the pre-1970s attitude, and included the following:

- deal with pollution at source;
- take environmental issues into account at the earliest stage;
- avoid abusive exploitation of natural resources;
- promote conservation and improve standard of knowledge;
- the polluter should pay for the damage they caused;
- activities in one state shouldn't degrade environment of another;
- have regard to developing countries;
- should be clear long-term EU environmental policy;
- environmental protection is for everybody;
- establish action levels for each type of pollution;
- harmonisation of environmental protection.

Many of these ideas are clearly forerunners of what we would today categorise as the precautionary, preventative or polluter pays principle (see below).

The current EAP (the sixth) is called Environment 2010: Our Future, Our Choice and was initially set to run from 2002 to 2010, but has subsequently been extended to 2012. It sets out actions, including calls to improve implementation of environmental legislation; integration of the environment into social and economic policies; and ownership of environmental protection efforts by stakeholders and citizens.

There is a seventh EAP ('Living well, within the limits of our planet') on the drawing board, which is set to last until 2020, although it has yet to be formally implemented. The three thematic priority objectives, published in November 2012, are intended to 'Protect nature and strengthen ecological resilience; Boost sustainable resource-efficient low-carbon growth, and Effectively address environment-related threats to health.' (DG Environment, 2012)

Single European Act 1986 (SEA) and Maastricht Treaty 1992 (or Treaty of the European Union (TEU))

Despite the EAPs, the purpose of environmental legislation until the SEA was to ensure that different environmental standards did not distort the operation of the market. However, the SEA inserted Articles 130R–130T (these are currently Arts. 191–193 of the Treaty on the Functioning of the European Union) into the Treaty. Article 191 sets out the objectives of EU policy, and Article 192 sets out the principles which should be applied in achieving these objectives. Broadly speaking, these principles are the preventive, precautionary, and polluter pays principles, and the wider principle of integration with other policies.

KEY STATUTE

Article 191 Treaty on the Functioning of the European Union

(1) Community policy on the environment shall contribute to pursuit of the following objectives:

- preserving, protecting and improving the quality of the environment,
- protecting human health,
- prudent and rational utilisation of natural resources,
- promoting measures at international level to deal with regional or worldwide environmental problem.

Article 191 goes on to say that policy will primarily be based on the precautionary principle (see below), but also on 'the principles that preventive action should be taken, that environmental damage should as a priority be rectified at source and that the polluter should pay' (Art. 191(2)).

By introducing the four Articles, the SEA also allowed for explicit law-making in environmental issues for the first time.

The Maastricht Treaty (TEU) took the work of the SEA further and re-stated Article 2 of the Treaty to include the phrases 'sustainable growth' and 'a high level of protection and improvement of the quality of the environment', adding Article 6 ('Environmental protection requirements must be integrated into the definition and implementation of the Community policies . . . with a view to promoting sustainable development').

KEY CASE

Commission v *Denmark,* Case 302/86 [1988] ECR 4607

Concerning: free movement of goods; environmental protection

Facts

Denmark introduced a regulation in 1981 which stated that all beer and soft drink containers must be returnable, and it was approved by the National Agency for the Protection of the Environment. The UK and the Commission argued this was a breach of Article 28 ('Quantitative restrictions on imports and all measures having equivalent effect shall be prohibited between Member States' – this is Article 34 TFEU).

Legal principle

Denmark lost the case, but the principle was established that it was permissible for a member state to use environmental protection as a justification for discriminating against foreign manufacturers (see also *France* v *Commission* Case C-41/93 [1994] ECR I-1829).

Domestic law

Although the guiding principles and wider direction of environmental law are set out by international and/or EU law, the vast majority of environmental law is given practical application by domestic law, either in the form of legislation or case law.

Legislation

Past legislation was piecemeal and lacking in structure, and was generally used to 'plug the gaps' left by case law (see Chapter 1). The real power of legislation, however, is to consolidate and codify the law. In land law, for example, this was done with the Law of Property Act 1925. It has only recently started to be done in environmental law, however, firstly with the Environmental Protection Act 1990 and Environment Act 1995, and more recently the Environmental Permitting Regulations 2010.

Once a piece of statute becomes law, that is not necessarily an end to its development, however, as many of the terms used will subsequently be interpreted by the courts in any relevant cases.

Statutory interpretation

There are three rules of statutory interpretation.

KEY DEFINITION: Rules of statutory interpretation

Literal rule: 'the objective of the court is to discover the intention of Parliament as expressed in the words used in the statute and nothing else' (*Stock* v *Frank Jones (Tipton) Ltd* [1978] 1 All ER 948, per Viscount Dilhorne at 951).

Golden rule: 'the grammatical and ordinary sense of the word is to be adhered to, unless that would lead to some absurdity, or some repugnance or inconsistency' (*John Grey and Others* v *William Pearson and Others* (1857) 6 HL Cas 61, per Wensleydale LJ at 106).

Mischief rule: Allows the court to base its interpretation on the 'mischief' which previous statute allowed, but which the current law was brought in to address.

In addition to these three rules, *Pepper (Inspector of Taxes)* v *Hart* [1993] AC 593 held that, where legislative wording was ambiguous or obscure, the prohibition on referring back to Parliamentary debates could be relaxed.

Case law

In England and Wales, the doctrine of precedent essentially provides that the decisions of higher courts are binding on future decisions of lower courts. This means that, unlike in international law, there is an ever-increasing body of case law which is binding on future decisions. A simplified diagram of the hierarchy of the courts is set out below.

Supreme Court (replaced House of Lords in 2009)

Court of Appeal

Divisional Court

High Court

Magistrates' Court/ Crown Court/ County Court

Case law reports are often extremely lengthy and can be difficult to navigate, and the key skill is to be able to distinguish between the *ratio decidendi* (the statement of the law by the court) and *obiter dicta* (other things said – in other words, everything which is not the *ratio*). The *ratio* is the statement of the law which is binding on any inferior courts, whereas the *obiter* is not binding (although it can be persuasive). To make things even trickier, a court will not say in the judgment which section is the *ratio*, and it is left to subsequent cases and legal scholars to interpret what the *ratio* of a particular case was.

Concepts

Sustainable development

The UNCHE 1972 recognised that there was a link between economic development and environmental protection ('The protection and improvement of the human environment is a major issue which affects the well-being of peoples and economic development throughout the world'), but the formal incorporation of the impact had still not been made by 1984, in the UN Resolution on the Charter of Economic Rights and Duties of States (A/RES/39/163).

In 1983 (A/RES/38/161), the UN convened the World Commission on Environment and Development (WCED, generally known as the Brundtland Commission). The commission reported in 1987 ('Our Common Future' or 'The Brundtland Report'), and the report pointed to the need to ensure sustainable development (SD) to provide mechanisms to increase international cooperation.

KEY DEFINITION: Sustainable development (SD)

Development that meets the needs of the present without compromising the ability of future generations to meet their own needs. It contains within it two key concepts:

- the concept of 'needs', in particular the essential needs of the world's poor, to which overriding priority should be given; and
- the idea of limitations imposed by the state of technology and social organisation on the environment's ability to meet present and future needs.

Sustainable development has several advantages as an approach – it considers environmental protection, but with the emphasis on economic and social development. It is also quite pragmatic, since it takes into account needs of the undeveloped and developing world, as well as the potential benefits and problems of technological advances.

Sustainable development has made the transition from a concept of international law (and thus soft law) to hard EU law in a remarkably short period. It was included as Agenda 21 of the UNCED 1992 and was incorporated into the EC Treaty in Article 2 ('a harmonious, balanced and sustainable development of economic activities . . .') and Article 6 ('Environmental protection requirements must be integrated into the definition and implementation of the Community policies and activities referred to in Article 3, in particular with a view to promoting sustainable development').

Sustainable development is not as straightforward as it might appear, however. One of its strengths as a soft law concept was that it can mean different things to different people (and so states could sign up to Agenda 21 and interpret the ideas as they wished).

In the UK, SD appears in statute several times, most recently in s. 110 of the Localism Act 2011 ('Duty to co-operate in relation to planning of sustainable development'). It also appears in the outline of the principal aims and objectives of the Environment Agency (s. 4(1) Environment Act 1995).

> **! Don't be tempted to . . .**
>
> Try not to think of SD as being a concrete set of rules that govern activities. Even in statute, the term is not defined consistently (if at all) and it is left to the courts to apply the most suitable definition of SD in any particular case.

The government's approach on SD has been criticised recently, however. The Environmental Audit Committee (see Chapter 4 on enforcement of environmental law) criticised the closure of the Sustainable Development Commission in March 2011, and says that since 2008 'policy on sustainable development has not been overseen by a designated ministerial committee' (EAC, 2011).

Precautionary principle

The precautionary principle, which evolved out of the German *Vorsorgeprinzip* or principle of anticipation through foresight, can be summarised as being 'an approach . . . that is based around taking precautions even if there is no clear evidence of harm or risk of harm from an activity or substance' (Bell, McGillivray and Pedersen, 2013: 68).

As a principle, it is open to a number of interpretations:

- The process or project should be allowed to proceed unless or until it is found to be damaging to the environment.
- The process or project should not be allowed to proceed unless or until it is found not to be damaging to the environment.

These could both be argued to represent the precautionary principle, but will clearly have dramatically different impacts on development.

The precautionary principle appears in EU law in Article 191(2) TFEU as one of the key principles upon which EU environmental policy will be based.

> **□ REVISION NOTE**
>
> One practical embodiment of the precautionary principle is illustrated in Chapter 5 (on planning) and Chapter 6 (on environmental permitting) as environmental impact assessments, which should be considered alongside the theory.

Polluter pays principle

The polluter pays principle (PPP) is probably one of the most widely recognised of the principles covered here.

KEY DEFINITION: Polluter pays principle (PPP)

The principle to be used for allocating costs of pollution prevention and control measures to encourage rational use of scarce environmental resources and to avoid distortion in international trade is the so-called 'polluter pays principle'.

This means that the polluters should bear the expenses of carrying out remediation measures decided by the public authorities (OECD Principle A(a)4, 1974).

Within EU law, the PPP was first mentioned as a principle in the 1st Environmental Action Programme in 1973, and is currently one of the key principles outlined in Article 191 of the TFEU.

Under the PPP, the polluter should pay the costs incurred through polluting activities, either directly or indirectly, using mechanisms such as:

- administration costs for pollution control system (licensing fees which pay for monitoring, for example);
- external costs – for example, landfill (through taxes); or
- clean-up costs (by setting requirements/standards in relation to polluting activity).

✎ EXAM TIP

Remember that large polluters are often multinational corporations, who will often try to offset the burden of paying for their pollution by reducing shareholder dividends, or raising prices. Since it is the shareholders and the customers who drive the corporation's business, could it be argued that even with this offsetting, the polluter is still paying? In other words, don't interpret 'the polluter' too narrowly in your answer.

Human right to a safe and healthy environment

If the three concepts above have evolved into more or less enforceable principles of environmental law, then there are also new concepts emerging that might in future become hard law. Key among these is the argument that certain aspects of the environment are so strongly connected with human rights that to damage the environment is to be in breach of a human right, either under the UDHR or ECHR.

This was brought up in the ECHR cases of *López Ostra* v *Spain* (1994) 20 EHRR 277 (where the state failed to close a polluting factory), *Fadeyeva* v *Russia* (2005) 45 EHRR 295 (where the state failed to relocate people affected by a noxious steel factory), and *Giacomelli* v *Italy* (2007) 45 EHRR 38 (the state had failed to close a polluting waste treatment plant). All of these cases involved a breach of Article 8 (the right to a family life). To date, only one environmental case has been found to be a breach of Article 2 (the right to life), and that was *Öneryildiz* v *Turkey* [2004] ECHR 657.

KEY CASE

Öneryildiz v *Turkey* (1994) ECHR 657

Concerning: hazardous pursuits; landfill sites; positive obligations; protection of property; right to effective remedy; right to life

Facts

The applicant lived in a slum quarter of Istanbul surrounding a rubbish tip which exploded because of the decomposition of the refuse and killed nine of his relatives. A report showed that the authorities failed to take any measures at the tip in question to prevent an explosion of methane.

Legal principle

The court noted that the regulatory framework applicable in the present case had proved defective in that the tip had been allowed to open and operate and there had been no coherent supervisory system. That situation had been exacerbated by a general policy which had proved powerless in dealing with general town-planning issues and had undoubtedly played a part in the sequence of events leading to the accident. The Court accordingly held that there had been a violation of Article 2.

Whether or not these four cases amount to the beginnings of a new concept of environmental law remains to be seen.

EXAM TIP

Consider what takes an idea from the abstract to concept to principle. At the moment, this is an organic process, but you would impress an examiner with a discussion about whether there should be a more prescriptive approach in developing new principles of law.

■ Putting it all together

Answer guidelines

See the essay question at the start of the chapter.

Approaching the question

The question asks you to consider the sources of environmental law and the level of impact that each might have. The broad nature of the question allows you to shape it along a direction that best suits your knowledge. You could look at this question in terms of 'environmental law' as a broad, single concept, or make the approach much more specific to one or two particular areas of law, for example, planning law and climate change. You should also spend a little time introducing the potential sources of law covered above.

Important points to include

- What area will you be focusing on?
- What are the sources of law? International/ EU/ domestic/ a combination of all of these? Has the law been developed in this area by the courts? How?
- (How) do they mesh together in relation to the area you have chosen?
- How 'effective' is the law in this area?
- Would this be improved if the law had originated from a different source?
- You might think about a comparison with another area of law here.

 Make your answer stand out

Make sure that you distinguish clearly between the different sources that might have impacted on the particular area of law that you are discussing. If it has emerged from soft law, for example, revisit the Blutman–Kaufmann–Kohler–Ellis–Barelli debates above. An analysis of this sort will ensure you get the best marks, whereas merely describing the various sources will not.

READ TO IMPRESS

Barelli, M. (2009) The role of soft law in the international legal system: the case of the United Nations Declaration on the Rights of Indigenous Peoples, *ICLQ* 58(4), 957–83

Barczewski, M. (2011) From hard to soft law: a requisite shift in the International copyright regime, *IIC* 42(1) 40–54

Bell, S., McGillivray, D. and Pedersen, O. (2013) *Environmental Law*, 8th Edn. Oxford: Oxford University Press

Birnie, P., Boyle, A. and Redgewell, C. (2009) *International Law and the Environment*, Oxford: OUP

Blutman, L. (2010) In the trap of a legal metaphor: international soft law, *ICLQ* 59(3), 605–24

Cassese, A. (2004) *International Law*, 2nd Edn. Oxford: Oxford University Press

Castro, C. (2004) Sustainable development: mainstream and critical perspectives, *Organization & Environment* 17(2), June, 195–225

Cook, K. (2010) The right to food and the environment, *Env. L. Rev.* 12(1), 1–11

EAC (2011) Embedding sustainable development across Government, after the Secretary of State's announcement on the future of the Sustainable Development Commission, Volume I, House of Commons Environmental Audit Committee Report HC504, London: TSO

Ellis, J. (2012) Shades of grey: soft law and the validity of public international law, *Leiden Journal of International Law*, 25(2), 313–334

Finch, E. and Fafinski, S. (2012) *Law Express: English Legal System*, Harlow: Pearson

Kaufmann-Kohler, G. (2010) Soft law in international arbitration: codification and normativity, *JIDS* 1(2), 283–99

Kirk, E. (2012) *Law Express: EU Law*, Harlow: Pearson

Morag-Levine, N. (2011) Is precautionary regulation a civil law instrument? Lessons from the history of the Alkali Act, *J. Env. L.* 23(1), 1–43

OECD (1974) *Environment and Economics Guiding Principles Concerning International Economic Aspects of Environmental Policies*, Paris: Organisation for Economic Cooperation and Development

PCA (2011) *About Us*, The Hague: Permanent Court of Arbitration

Vinuales, J. E. (2011) Balancing effectiveness and fairness in the redesign of the climate change regime, *LJIL* 24(1), 223–52

www.pearsoned.co.uk/lawexpress

Go online to access more revision support including quizzes to test your knowledge, sample questions with answer guidelines, podcasts you can download, and more!

Enforcement of environmental law

4

Revision checklist

Essential points you should know:

- [ ] Who the policy-making bodies are
- [ ] The role of local authorities
- [ ] The role of the Environment Agency (EA)
- [ ] The key differences and aspects of direct and indirect regulation
- [ ] The importance of access to environmental information and judicial review

■ Topic map

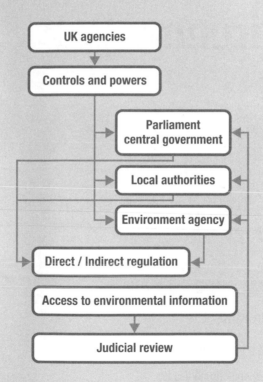

■ Introduction

Many exam questions will want you to focus on the enforcement of environmental law, as this is often regarded as the weakest link (de Prez, 2000; CCG, 2004).

The origins and development of environmental law, as well as some of the underlying principles upon which it is based, have been explored in other chapters, but we will now turn to the regulatory systems in place for environmental law, focusing on the UK. The specific aspects of enforcement and regulation with respect to, say, planning law, will be dealt with in more detail later (see Chapter 5, and so on).

This is a topic area which is most likely to come up in conjunction with something else. However, this is not to say that it cannot come up on its own, and you should be prepared to answer such a question should it arise.

Essay questions

Given the recent changes in government and legislation, an essay question is likely to involve an analysis of the impact of the recent changes on the enforcing bodies.

Problem questions

These could be based on a scenario with different regulators potentially being involved. You will need to consider the remit of the different organisations and the sanctions that are available.

■ Sample question

Could you answer this question? Below is a typical essay question that could arise on this topic. Guidelines on answering the question are included at the end of this chapter, whilst a sample problem question and guidance on tackling it can be found on the companion website.

To what extent will the creation of Natural Resources Wales in 2013 affect the regulation of the environment?

◼ UK agencies

One of the perennial issues about the enforcement of environmental law is that of responsibility. Under the early legal systems outlined in the previous chapters, when environmental law was in its infancy, this was a relatively easy problem to solve as, with tort being the primary mechanism available, the injured party was primarily responsible for bringing an action. Today, the system is much more complex, and the key elements of it will be outlined below, with the caveat above concerning specific enforcement actions.

One aspect which unites the various enforcement bodies is their objectives, which can generally be separated into four main categories:

- controlling pollution by licences and authorisations (e.g. waste management licences, water discharge consents, and environmental permits);
- monitoring and enforcing compliance with environmental controls;
- enforcing statutory controls;
- giving advice and undertaking research.

There will inevitably be overlap between these categories, and also between the roles played by the different enforcement bodies, but whether the action originates with central government, local authorities or the Environment Agency, it will fit into one or more of the categories above.

Policy-making bodies

House of Commons Environmental Audit Committee (EAC)

The EAC, which is a cross-party committee (i.e. it draws members from all political parties), does not look at the work of a specific government department, which most select committees do, but instead 'considers the extent to which the policies and programmes of government departments and non-departmental public bodies contribute to environmental protection and sustainable development' (Parliament, 2012). This role, combined with its role as an auditor of 'performance against any sustainable development and environmental protection targets' (Parliament, 2012) means that it has a wide-reaching impact both on policy and on implementation of policy.

Within government, there are three main departments whose work has a direct bearing on the environment. Each of these is mirrored by a House of Commons Select Committee, which will examine the expenditure, administration and policy of the relevant department.

Environment, Food and Rural Affairs

The Department of the Environment, Food and Rural Affairs (Defra), describes itself as 'the UK government department responsible for policy and regulations on the environment, food and rural issues' (Defra, 2013). It is the major player of the government departments, and has influence on the widest range of environmental policy.

Energy and Climate Change

As can be expected from its name, the Department of Energy and Climate Change (DECC) has very specific responsibility for policy and legislation developments in the related areas of energy efficiency and the implications for climate change.

Communities and Local Government

The Department of Communities and Local Government (DCLG) has an influence on environmental policy under the banner of 'planning, building and the environment'. The planning implications of the work of DCLG will be discussed later (see Chapter 5).

Other bodies

In addition to the government departments that have an influence in the different aspects of environmental law, there are several bodies which have existed to advise and inform government environmental policy. Key among these was the Royal Commission on Environmental Pollution (RCEP), which was set up in 1970, and produced a number of reports on different aspects of the environment. RCEP, which was paid for by Defra, was subjected to a review in 2007, which found that it was 'broadly fit for purpose', but in need of modernisation (Defra, 2007).

A more recent body was the Sustainable Development Commission, which was created in June 2000 to advise the central and devolved governments on issues pertaining to sustainable development (see Chapter 3 on sources and concepts of environmental law). As with the RCEP, the SDC was paid for by Defra, who ceased funding in June 2010. On 22 July 2010, the Secretary of State for the Environment, Food and Rural Affairs announced that both the RCEP and SDC would be closed down by the government in March 2011, along with the Inland Waterways Advisory Council. The closures have been criticised widely. The EAC recommended that the effects of the closure of the SDC were mitigated by the creation of a Minister for Sustainable Development (EAC, 2011: pp. 4, 18).

Other bodies which play a role in relation to specific areas include Natural England (see Chapter 10 on nature conservation and landscape management), which describes itself as 'the government's advisor on the natural environment' (NE, 2013) and the newly formed Marine Management Organisation, which has 'incorporated the work of the Marine and Fisheries Agency (MFA) and acquired several important new roles, principally marine-related powers and specific functions previously associated with the DECC and the Department for Transport (DfT)' (MMO, 2013).

> ✎ EXAM TIP
>
> If an exam question asks you to examine the impact of recent policy decisions on enforcement, remember to look at the wider picture, and that formal enforcement is often not the most cost-effective method of remedying damage.

Local authorities

Although central government has the responsibility for setting policy on the environment, a large proportion of the enforcement and implementation of these policies rests with the local authorities, which have a wide range of responsibilities and powers. These include the following:

- planning control;
- building control;
- waste management;
- regulating processes under Part A2 and Part B of the Environmental Permitting Regulations 2010.

> **📖 REVISION NOTE**
>
> You might find it useful to draw a mind map outlining the areas of responsibility that the different regulators have. Remember that the list above is not exhaustive and that there will also be specific regulators which are relevant in the areas covered in the following chapters.

The Environment Agency (EA)

The Environment Act 1995 created two new enforcement bodies, the Environment Agency and the Scottish Environmental Protection Agency, which came into being on 1 April 1996. The two agencies took over the work of Her Majesty's Inspectorate of Pollution (HMIP, which had been created in 1987) and the National Rivers Authority (NRA, created in 1989). They also took on some of the work of the local authorities in relation to waste management and waste regulation. In Northern Ireland, the equivalent role is played by the Northern Ireland Environment Agency, which is a part of the Department of the Environment Northern Ireland.

The EA describes its principal aims as being to 'protect and improve the environment, and to promote sustainable development' (EA, 2013). It is worth noting here that under the draft National Assembly for Wales (Legislative Competence) (Environment) Order 2010, the functions of the Environment Agency in Wales may come under the remit of the Welsh Assembly.

The duty of the Agency was set out in s. 7 of the Environment Act 1995. It is clear to see that the role of the agency was balanced between 'conservation and enhancement' on the one hand, and 'economic and social well-being' on the other. In practice this meant that the EA would undertake an impact assessment (either economic or environmental, or both) before carrying out many of its roles.

Section 7 Environment Act 1995

(1) . . .

  (a) . . . to further the conservation and enhancement of natural beauty and the conservation of flora, fauna and geological or physiographical features of special interest;

  (b) . . .

  (c) any proposal relating to any functions of the Agency –

   (i) to have regard to the desirability of protecting and conserving buildings, sites and objects of archaeological, architectural, engineering or historic interest;

   (ii) to take into account any effect which the proposals would have on the beauty or amenity of any rural or urban area or on any such flora, fauna, features, buildings, sites or objects; and

   (iii) to have regard to any effect which the proposals would have on the economic and social well-being of local communities in rural areas.

The EA (along with Natural England) was one of the first regulatory bodies to be granted additional powers under the Regulatory Enforcement and Sanctions Act 2008. The powers were established by the Environmental Civil Sanctions (England) Order 2010. The range of sanctions made available under the Regulations includes fixed and variable monetary penalties, **compliance notices**, **restoration notices**, third-party undertakings and **stop notices**. To date, the EA has not exercised any of these powers, which are additional to its existing range of powers.

In April 2013, a new body – Natural Resources Wales – was created, and took over the work of the Countryside Council for Wales, Environment Agency Wales and Forestry Commission Wales. This means that there are now different enforcement bodies in England, Wales, Scotland and Northern Ireland.

KEY DEFINITION: Compliance, restoration and stop notices

Compliance notice: Specifies the steps a person needs to undertake to secure that the offence to which the notice relates does not continue or recur.

Restoration notice: Specifies the steps a person needs to undertake, and the period in which they must be taken, to secure that the position is, so far as possible, restored to what it would have been if the offence had not been committed.

Stop notice: Prohibits a person from carrying on an activity specified in the notice until the person has taken the steps specified in the notice.

The bodies covered above all play a role in drafting policy and setting standards to ensure fairness and consistency in enforcement. They can do this through direct or indirect enforcement.

▮ Direct regulation

As a general category, direct regulation is sometimes called the 'command and control' regime, where standards are set, as are penalties for failing to meet them. There are several ways of drafting direct regulation, and often they are used conjunctively.

Environmental quality standards (EQS)

EQS (also referred to as target standards), are set to ensure that a certain effect does or does not occur. The standard usually relates to a measurable quality in relation to the receiving environmental medium (i.e. air, water, land) and/or in a particular geographical area. As the EQS concentrate on the receiving environment, the standards can be set to allow review of all possible pathways and all possible pollutants, and can also be applied differently from area to area depending on demands or sensitivity of those areas.

The standards are generally expressed in terms of limit values and target values. Limit values are those which must not be exceeded (other than as specified in the relevant legislation) and target values, which are more aspirational in character. As Wilde (2010: 285) puts it (in relation to Directive 2008/50/EC on ambient air quality and cleaner air for Europe):

> Whilst there is no specific penalty for exceeding a target value per se, the Member State must show that it aspires to this objective and has plans in place to achieve it. Target values are typically used where there is scientific uncertainty regarding what levels are acceptable (if at all), or where it has not been possible to achieve political consensus.

Examples of EQS include the Air Quality Standards Regulations 2010, which set out the limit value (Sch. 2) and target values (Sch. 3) for a number of air pollutants and, more widely, the Environmental Permitting (England and Wales) Regulations 2010 ('the Permitting Regulations').

Emission standards (ES)

ES (also referred to as emission limit values (ELV)) relate to measurable quantities of substances emitted from a particular source – a pipe or a chimney, for example. As with EQS, they are usually expressed as maximum or minimum concentrations of substances or noise and, as they relate to a particular polluter and their emissions, they are conceptually relatively easily controlled and monitored.

The overall standard can be gradually improved by requiring polluters to decrease harmful pollutants. One example of this is the requirement for the **'best available technique'** (BAT) under the permitting regulations, which means that every time a permit needs renewing, the standard could be higher.

It is also practically easier to enforce ES, since it is the emissions from each polluter that are being monitored, and thus if the polluter fails to reach the set standard, they are open to prosecution.

EQS v ES

Drawbacks of using EQS	Drawbacks of using ES
Need constant monitoring	Diffuse pollution is much more difficult to control
Hard to raise standard in relation to one specific polluter	Hard to control an accumulative effect of pollutants if individual emissions are all within the standard set
May be difficult or impossible to identify an excessive polluter where there are many potential polluters and so may be difficult to enforce the standard	

Both EQS and ES are effectively reactive in nature – there may be elements of proactivity in terms of setting standards and so on, but both sets of standard are based on allowing polluters to pollute (following a suitable risk assessment) and then keeping that pollution at a manageable level – i.e. a level at which there is no deleterious effect on the environment.

EXAM TIP

A question may want you to explore the relationship between EQS and ES, so remember that they are not mutually exclusive, and are often used in conjunction.

Process standards

Process standards are directly aimed at regulating the processes which give rise to pollution. They may stipulate that a particular process is used to achieve a particular outcome, or set a performance standard in relation to certain types of equipment.

Process standards may relate to the whole or a part of the process, the method of the process and the technology to be used. Bell, McGillivray and Pedersen give as an example of process standards 'a requirement that Best Available Techniques (BAT) are used to prevent environmental harm (although the general requirement is often, in practice, translated into a set of emission standards in order to achieve environmental quality standards' (p. 242).

Use standards

As the name suggests, use standards relate to the way that a particular product or series of products is used, rather than any aspect of the manufacturing process. One example of this is the REACH (registration, evaluation, authorisation and restriction of chemicals) system imposed under EU Regulation 1907/2006, Article 1(3), which states 'it is for manufacturers, importers and downstream users to ensure that they manufacture, place on the market or use such substances that do not adversely affect human health or the environment'. Use standards can link to EQS, such as the use of priority substance lists in the Water Framework Directive 2000/60/EC (see Chapter 8 on water pollution).

□ REVISION NOTE

Keep these types of standard in mind when looking at the subject matter covered in other chapters in this guide. As you go through, make a note of whether you think that standards used in, say, environmental permitting (Chapter 6) are EQS, ES, process or use standards. You can then use those examples to enrich your answer.

Applying direct standards

With the exception of use standards, direct standards are generally applied reactively – in other words, the person wanting to carry out a particular activity must first apply to a particular body for permission to do so. The body, which in the majority of cases in England and Wales will be the Environment Agency, will then deal with the application in two stages.

Authorisation

Depending upon the type of pollutant or process, the level of prohibition will differ:

- absolute prohibition;
- prohibition unless discretionary consent/licence/permit is granted;
- prohibition without registration – permits are automatically granted on registration;
- prohibition without notification to a specified body which is responsible for monitoring.

For example, an application to produce chlorofluorocarbons (CFCs) would be under the 'absolute prohibition' category, because the UK is a signatory to the 1985 Vienna Convention on Substances that Deplete the Ozone Layer, which bans the production of such chemicals.

An application to become a registered waste carrier (upper or lower tier – see Chapter 9 on waste management) on the other hand would need consent to be granted by the Environment Agency, which would consider a number of factors before allowing the applicant to register.

Monitoring

Once permission has been granted (whether conditional or unconditional), the Agency must still monitor the process, to ensure that the terms of the permission are being adhered to. This can be done through inspections, notices to comply and ultimately prosecution in a number of cases.

The UK has traditionally favoured a more informal, compliance-based, approach to regulation, but EU regulations are moving towards a sanction-based approach.

Effects of direct standards

Pollution ends up being reduced to 'acceptable levels', not as far as possible – the stance has always been that pollution is relative and cannot be eradicated completely.

 Make your answer stand out

On this point of the pragmatic approach to pollution reduction, consider the criticism which has been levelled at the Comprehensive Environmental Response Compensation and Liability Act 1980 ('Superfund Act') in the United States, under which potentially responsible persons were subjected to a tax levy to clear up contaminated sites. US Congress argued for 'taxes . . . high enough to reduce pollution to zero' (in 1971) since that was the ultimate goal. As at May 2013, The Superfund, described as a 'disaster' by President Clinton in 1996, has cleaned up 365 sites in 33 years, and has 1,320 sites remaining (EPA, 2013).

The UK's approach has traditionally been reactive, rather than anticipatory, and fragmented, rather than integrated, but this has changed over recent years, with the centralisation of agencies (the EA, Health and Safety Executive and Health Protection Agency have taken on the roles of many smaller agencies). EU policy and environmental standards are also guiding UK policy, and this has driven the change to a more integrated and proactive approach.

Local authorities still retain *most* powers, but imposition of National Strategic Policy documents from central government (e.g. on waste, air quality) has reduced their discretion.

■ Indirect regulation

Whereas direct regulations focus on the polluting activity itself, indirect regulation tends to centre on economic instruments, the effect of which will be to impose a higher burden on higher polluters. As such, they are based on the polluter pays principle (see Chapter 3 on sources and concepts of environmental law). Examples include the following:

■ charge for regulatory system;

■ application costs, licence fees, annual monitoring charges, etc.;

■ charge for environmental cost;

■ taxes on external costs (those not reflected in production or provision costs of goods or services) on goods having adverse effects;

■ charge for polluting activity;

■ fines following prosecution, or taxing a polluting activity to discourage it.

Using the funds

The money generated from indirect regulation is generally dealt with in one of three ways:

■ In most cases, the money returns to central government, and is then used to fund general government spending.

■ Sometimes, the money is 'ring-fenced' for specific environmental purposes. The Landfill Tax allowed landfill operators to offset some of the tax for which they were liable to fund environmental projects under the Landfill Tax Credit Scheme (now Landfill Communities Fund, LCF).

■ In rarer cases the money may be used to finance the relevant system, and this is the case for the licensing regime relating to houses in multiple occupancy in Scotland under the Civic Government (Scotland) Act 1982 (Licensing of Houses in Multiple Occupation) Order 2000.

Self-regulation

In the era of increasing corporate social responsibility many companies are choosing to apply for voluntary management standards which then tie them in to certain levels of performance. Probably the best known of these are the ISO 14000 Environmental Management Standard, and the European Eco-Management and Audit Scheme (EMAS), which are entirely voluntary (but to qualify for which companies must undergo an annual audit of their environmental management systems).

Other companies prefer to adopt their own environmental standards, which are a lot more flexible and non-interventionist in nature, although these are often criticised for having vague standards and for being unaccountable, with no realistic enforcement system.

> **! Don't be tempted to . . .**
>
> Don't assume that all voluntary or self-imposed regulation is a poor substitute for external regulation. Many of the voluntary environmental standards and schemes (Fair Trade, Rainforest Alliance, etc.) are highly developed and well respected.

■ Access to environmental information and judicial review

Whichever is used, it is vital that the system is transparent, and is *seen* to operate fairly (almost as important as *actually* operating fairly). The EU reporting-back requirements (on implementation of laws) is often mechanistic, and is also often assessed by the body that is implementing it. Under the IPPC scheme, for example, the EA was responsible for ensuring that the system was working properly, and for reporting back to government on its progress. Access to environmental information through the large number of open-access environmental registers and informal monitoring through academic research are thus extremely important in this area.

Access to information

Sir Francis Bacon is alleged to have said, 'scientia potentia est' (knowledge is power) and, whether the phrase is attributable to him or not, it remains true. Early steps in requiring the dissemination of environmental information were laid down in Directive 90/313/EEC on the freedom of access to information on the environment, which imposed a duty on public bodies to give information on the following areas:

- ■ state of water, air, flora, fauna, soil, natural site or other land;
- ■ activities giving rise to noise or other nuisance adversely affecting anything listed above;
- ■ activities to protect anything listed above.

The Directive has subsequently been replaced by Directive 2003/4/EC on public access to environmental information, which sets out its objectives in Article 1.

KEY STATUTE

Directive 2003/4/EC on public access to environmental information), Article 1 (Objectives)

The objectives of this Directive are:

(a) to guarantee the right of access to environmental information held by or for public authorities and to set out the basic terms and conditions of, and practical arrangements for, its exercise; and ▶

> (b) to ensure that, as a matter of course, environmental information is progressively made available and disseminated to the public in order to achieve the widest possible systematic availability and dissemination to the public of environmental information. To this end the use, in particular, of computer telecommunication and/or electronic technology, where available, shall be promoted.

The Directive carries on to insist that 'Member States shall ensure that public authorities are required, in accordance with the provisions of this Directive, to make available environmental information held by or for them to any applicant at his request and without his having to state an interest' (Art. 3). The Directive was transposed into English law by the Environmental Information Regulations 2004.

Judicial review

Public authorities sometimes make rulings that are wrong in law, contrary to natural justice or *ultra vires* (beyond their powers). If they do, then the person against whom the decision has been made can apply for judicial review. This is a well-established area of law, and is discussed in Chapter 9 of Chris Taylor's *Constitutional and Administrative Law* (2009).

The problem of judicial review for environmental cases is sometimes that of proving sufficient *locus standi* – i.e. a sufficient interest in the case. This requirement exists as a way of preventing people from interfering with cases and decisions which did not concern or affect them. The courts have granted some NGOs *locus standi* in environmental cases (see the Key Case, below), and may be willing to continue, but it is hard for NGOs to prove they have it, and expensive to bring the action. Despite the judgment of the *Greenpeace* case, Otton J emphasised that 'This will have to be a matter to be considered on a case by case basis' (p. 102) and did not confer an automatic right on NGOs to bring an action in judicial review. Even if the hurdle of *locus standi* can be overcome, there are still significant issues of cost and delay associated with judicial review.

KEY CASE

R v HM Inspectorate of Pollution, ex parte Greenpeace (No. 2) [1994] 4 All ER 329; [1994] Env LR 76

Concerning: environmental law; judicial review; locus standi; *nuclear waste; pressure groups*

Facts

Greenpeace challenged a decision which allowed British Nuclear Fuels Ltd to operate the THORP nuclear reprocessing plant at Sellafield on the basis that HMIP and MAFF were acting *ultra vires*. BNFL argued that Greenpeace did not have sufficient *locus standi* to bring the case.

> **Legal principle**
>
> Greenpeace did have sufficient *locus standi* to bring the cases as, per Otton J, it was 'an entirely responsible and respected body with a genuine concern for the environment' (p. 100). The application was dismissed on the grounds that HMIP and MAFF were not acting *ultra vires*.

■ Putting it all together

Answer guidelines

See the essay question at the start of the chapter.

Approaching the question

The start to this question is straightforward enough, as you will need to look at the Environment Act 1995, and the powers that were conferred on the Environment Agency by it. In addition, you will need to consider the powers that the Environment Agency had prior to the Act, as this gives you a baseline against which you can measure the changes. Also consider that the new body incorporates the enforcement powers of the Countryside Council and Forestry Commission in Wales, and thus has a wider remit than you might at first think.

Important points to include

- Start off with the Act – why was it passed? What was it meant to do? Was it intended for environmental use? These are all things that have been covered in journals.
- Look at any criticisms of the Environment Agency that pre-dated the Act. The 2007 Pitt Review, for example, said that the Agency was 'not transparent enough' in its work on preventing flooding (p. 119). How would the new powers address these criticisms, if at all?
- It is too early to pass any concrete judgement on Natural Resources Wales, so you could use the separation between the EA in England and SEPA in Scotland as the basis for a comparison.

▶

Make your answer stand out

You could look at the issue of what makes an effective regulator, and how this is measured. Is it a case of the more prosecutions the better, or could lower levels of action be argued to illustrate a more effective way of working?.

READ TO IMPRESS

Bell, S., McGillivray D., and Pedersen, O. (2013) *Environmental Law*, 8th Edn. Oxford: Oxford University Press

CCG (2004) *Strengthening the Weakest Links: Strategies for Improving the Enforcement of Environmental Laws Globally*, Washington, DC: Center for Conservation and Government

Defra (2007) *Review of the Royal Commission on Environmental Pollution: consultant's report*, London: Department for Environment Food and Rural Affairs

Defra (2013) https://www.gov.uk/government/organisations/department-for-environment-food-rural-affairs

de Prez, P. (2000) Excuses, excuses: the ritual trivialisation of environmental prosecutions, *J. Env L.* 12(1), 65–77

EA (2013) What We Do, Environment Agency, http://www.environment-agency.gov.uk/aboutus/149356.aspx

EAC (2011) Embedding sustainable development across Government, after the Secretary of State's announcement on the future of the Sustainable Development Commission, Volume I, House of Commons Environmental Audit Committee Report HC504, London: TSO

EPA (2013) *National Priorities List (NPL)*, Washington, DC: US Environmental Protection Agency

Gunningham, N. (2009) Environment law, regulation and governance: shifting architectures, *J. Env L.* 2192, 179–212

Harrington, W. and Morgernstern, R. D. (2004) Economic incentives versus command and control: what's the best approach for solving environmental problems? *Resources* 152, 13–17

Kirk, E. and Blackstock, K. (2011) Enhanced decision making: balancing public participation against 'better regulation' in British environmental permitting regimes, *J. Env L.* 23(1), 97–116

Lowther, J. (2010) Making environmental law more effective? The Regulatory Enforcement and Sanctions Act 2005 and Enforcement of environmental offences, *Student Law Review* 61, 19–21

Macrory, R. (2009) *Regulation, Enforcement and Governance in Environmental Law*, Oxford: Hart

MMO (2013) About Us, Marine Management Organisation, http://marinemanagement.org.uk/about/index.htm

NE (2013) What we do, Natural England, www.naturalengland.org.uk/about_us/whatwedo/default.aspx

Parliament (2012) The Environmental Audit Committee, www.parliament.uk/eacom

Pitt, M., 2007, *Learning the Lessons from the 2007 Floods*, London: HMSO

Taylor, C. (2009) *Law Express: Constitutional and Administrative Law*, Harlow: Pearson

Wilde, M. (2010) The new Directive on ambient air quality and cleaner air for Europe, *Env. L. Rev.* 12(4), 282–290

www.pearsoned.co.uk/lawexpress

Go online to access more revision support including quizzes to test your knowledge, sample questions with answer guidelines, podcasts you can download, and more!

Planning law

Revision checklist

Essential points you should know:

☐ Operation of planning control (e.g. how use classes orders, general development orders and special development orders work)

☐ The development plan

☐ The process of applying for planning permission

☐ Environmental impact assessment

■ Topic map

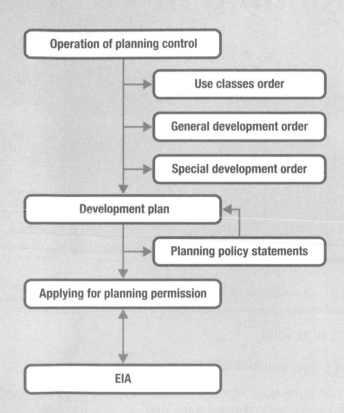

Operation of planning control

Use classes order

General development order

Special development order

Development plan

Planning policy statements

Applying for planning permission

EIA

■ Introduction

Exam questions about planning law concern a system that is vital to the way we live.

England is among the most crowded countries in the world, with approximately 90 per cent of the population living in urban areas which cover less than 10 per cent of the country. This makes decisions about how land is going to be used vital, not just because of the potential for increased risks to human life (e.g. flooding) but also because of the impact that development will have on the environment as a whole.

As seen in Chapter 1, some of the earliest of what would now be classed as environmental laws were passed in the nineteenth century as public health legislation, to try and remedy the worst effects of the unsanitary conditions that existed in some urban areas. In 1909, legislation was for the first time introduced to deal with other problems of land use. The Housing, Town Planning, etc. Act 1909 forbade, among other things, the building of new 'back-to-back' houses, and made provision for the preparation of planning schemes by councils for 'any land which is in course of development or appears likely to be used for building purposes' (Duxbury, 2006: 3). The Act also added requirements for planning control to relate to 'amenity and convenience' as well as public health.

The current system of planning control, which has its more direct roots in the Town and Country Planning Act 1990 (TCPA, 1990), has developed into a highly sophisticated system of planning control, and a process which deals not only with the initial use of land (which has remained in place for over a century) but also with *material change of use* and aspects of development design.

ASSESSMENT ADVICE

Essay questions

Essay questions on planning are likely to look at the more theoretical aspects of the topic – the links to sustainable development, for example, or the impact on energy policy. If this is the case, remember to make the planning aspects of your answer the primary focus.

Problem questions

A problem question will most likely take the form of a scenario with various actions that may or may not be classed as development. Watch out for any mention of a specific type of planning area – whether the question is set in a National Park, or Unitary Authority area, for example – as this may impact on the responsibilities and requirements.

■ Sample question

Could you answer this question? Below is a typical problem question that could arise on this topic. Guidelines on answering the question are included at the end of this chapter, whilst a sample essay question and guidance on tackling it can be found on the companion website.

PROBLEM QUESTION

James is a local businessman who owns a large industrial site, much of which is vacant.

There is a small factory on the site which assembles computer equipment. James wishes to change the use of the factory to assembly of audio equipment, and also expand the canteen used by his employees and convert it into a restaurant, to which the public will have access.

Until five years ago, he used a corner of the site for the storage and sale of second-hand cars. Since then, that part of the site has been totally unused, and now he wants to use it to store and sell second-hand cars once more.

In another corner of the site, which he has never put to any use, he wants to dig a pit, to be used for the storage of large wooden crates of fireworks, which will rest on concrete blocks.

By the main entrance to the site he wants to erect a 5-metre high, 10-metre wide advertising hoarding, bearing the company logo. The hoarding will be floodlit at night.

Advise James as to which of his proposals, if any, will need planning permission, and what steps he will need to take to obtain this permission.

■ The operation of planning control

A simple explanation of planning control is that a person who wants to carry out development must submit an application for planning permission to the local planning authority (LPA) before that development can take place. There are some circumstances where retrospective planning permission can be granted but this is not the norm.

The LPA will consider the application in the light of the development plan, and then make a decision whether to approve, reject, or conditionally approve the application. There is a route of appeal to the Planning Inspectorate and ultimately to the Secretary of State for Communities and Local Government, whose Department oversees the whole planning process.

> **! Don't be tempted to . . .**
>
> It is important to keep in mind throughout this topic area that even though a grant of planning permission can have an impact on the design and aesthetics of building, there is a significant difference between planning permission and building regulations.

One potential problem with this planning system is already apparent – there is involvement and input from the applicant, the LPA, the Department for Communities and Local Government, the Secretary of State and the Planning Inspectorate. These bodies and individuals will have to interpret various government policies and the implications of the relevant development plan (see below). A general rule is that the more complex a system is, the slower to navigate, and the slower to navigate, the more expensive it is. McEldowney and McEldowney (2010) point out, however, that '71 per cent of planning decisions on major application were made within 13 weeks' (p. 195), and this echoes what the Barker Review of Land Use Planning discovered in 2006, that the number of applications was higher in 2004–05 than in 1988–89 by around 50,000, and the percentage decided within eight weeks had also risen, to 76 per cent (p. 188, chart 1).

Of course, a decision will only need to be made by the LPA if planning permission is required, and that is restricted to cases where there is **development.**

KEY DEFINITION: Development

'The carrying out of building, engineering mining or other operations in, on, over or under land or making of any material change in the use of any buildings or other land' (s. 55(1) TCPA 1990).

Neither of the two aspects of development, namely operational development and material change of use, was newly introduced by the TCPA 1990 and, as Bell, McGillivray and Pedersen (2013) state, 'the basic structure of much of this system . . . has remained unchanged since then [the Town and Country Planning Act 1947], although the way in which it operates has, in practice, changed quite radically' (p. 406).

Operational development was further defined by s. 13(1) of the Planning and Compensation Act 1991, which inserted s. 1A into s. 55 TCPA 1990, stating that building operations included demolition, rebuilding or structural alterations of, or additions to buildings, and 'other operations normally undertaken by a person carrying on business as a builder' (s. 55(1A)(d) TCPA 1990).

It has been long established that the question as to whether something is a material change of use is 'a question of fact and degree in every case' (*East Barnet Urban District Council* v *British Transport Commission and Another* [1962] 2 QB 484 per Parker CJ at 492).

Because of the complex nature of planning permission, various attempts have been made over the years to streamline the process. Two of the key elements are use classes orders and general development orders.

 Make your answer stand out

There have been some discussions recently about the lack of certainty surrounding 'material change of use'. See, for example, Humphreys (2011), who finishes by saying, 'After over 60 years of the present concept of "development", it is surely time for clarity.' Use this to impress the examiners by discussing whether 'material change of use' ought to still be 'a question of fact and degree in every case' or whether it should be defined by statute.

KEY CASE

R (on the application Prudential Assurance Company Ltd) v Sunderland City Council [2010] EWHC 1771 (Admin)

Concerning: planning permission

Facts

The Prudential wanted to undertake internal and external alterations to buildings, and a dispute arose as to what the planning permission did and did not cover.

Legal principle

For the purposes of deciding whether a development fits within the s. 55 TCPA definition, 'It seems . . . wholly artificial to consider whether individual aspects of a development scheme, if standing alone, would or would not constitute development' per Wyn Williams J.

Use classes orders (UCO)

Introduced by the Town and Country Planning (Use Classes) Order 1987, the purpose of the provision was to classify uses of land into a number of different classes. In this way, if a developer wanted to change the use of a property (and not carry out any operational development), as long as the proposed use was within the same class as the existing use, no planning permission would be required. Article 3(1) of the Order states: 'where a building or other land is used for a purpose of any class specified in the Schedule, the use of that building or that other land for any other purpose of the same class shall not be taken to involve development of the land.'

Not all uses of land are covered, and these are listed in Article 3(6) of the Order.

Use classes

Class	Use
A1	Shops (not food)
A2	Financial and professional services
A3	Food and drink
A4	Drinking establishments
A5	Hot food takeaways
B1	Business
B2	General industrial
B8	Storage or distribution
C1	Hotels and hostels
C2	Residential institutions
C2A	Secure residential institutions
C3	Dwelling houses
C4	Houses in multiple occupation
D1	Non-residential institutions
D2	Assembly and leisure

General development orders (GDO)

In addition to the UCO, which effectively excuse actions which could otherwise have counted as 'material change of use' (and thus development), the Town and Country Planning (General Permitted Development) Order 1995 lists various classes of 'operational development' which are exempted from the requirements of planning permission.

The full list is in Schedule 2 to the Order, and it is important to remember that this is a general development order, rather than an absolute development order – in other words, even if development comes within one of the categories, there are still some restrictions in place.

Special development orders (SDO)

These were introduced by s. 59(3)(b) of the TCPA 1990, which states that development orders can be general, and apply to all land, or 'as a special order applicable only to such land or descriptions of land as may be specified in the order'. The SDO will be made in respect to a particular geographic area, and will only apply to specified types of development in that area.

✎ EXAM TIP

If a question asks you to discuss the impact of UCO/GDO/SDO on the planning system, think about how they could impact on wider policy issues such as the need for more housing, or inner-city redevelopment.

■ The development plan

Until the Planning and Compulsory Purchase Act 2004 (PCPA 2004), the decisions of the LPA had to have regard to, and be made in accordance with, the relevant development plan, creation of which was a requirement of the county, district or unitary authority.

The PCPA 2004 abolished the requirement for a development plan of the previous type, and replaced it with a number of regional spatial strategies (RSS) which would control regional planning bodies (RPB).

The Planning Act 2008 made further changes to the planning regulations for 'major infrastructure projects' and created different regimes for 'major' and 'nationally significant' infrastructure projects. The former will still be 'called in' for a decision by the Secretary of State, and the latter would be overseen by a new Infrastructure Planning Commission (IPC), created in 2009. Nationally significant infrastructure projects are those such as wind farms, power stations, major road and rail projects, waste and waste water.

The Local Democracy, Economic Development and Construction Act 2009 also made some changes to the planning system, and merged the RSS for each region with the regional economic strategy to create new regional strategies.

Section 128 of the Localism Act 2011, which received Royal Assent in November 2011, will replace the IPC with a Major Infrastructure Planning Unit (MIPU) that will report to the Secretary of State 'with the policy responsibility for the relevant industry sector' (DCLG, 2010: 5). The MIPU is also set to absorb the Planning Inspectorate. The Localism Act is also set to abolish the RSS, the RPB and the regional strategies.

Planning policy statements (PPS)

The DCLG put plans for a new National Planning Policy Framework out for public consultation in 2011 (DCLG, 2011). The new framework replaced all of the existing Planning Policy Statements, Mineral Planning Policy Guidance notes and the Marine Mineral Guidance Note with 'a simple and consolidated national planning framework covering all forms of development and setting out national economic, environmental and social priorities' (DCLG, 2011).

All of the topics covered in this section have been intended to make the planning system simpler and quicker (and less expensive). If a question gives you scope to do so, you could address whether the new changes are likely to make any appreciable difference to the existing system – would a single Planning Policy Framework help or hinder the objectives of planning, for example?

Applying for planning permission

In order to obtain planning permission, potential developers must follow a set procedure, set out under the Town and Country Planning (Development Management Procedure) (England) Order 2010. This is set out in Figure 5.1.

Figure 5.1

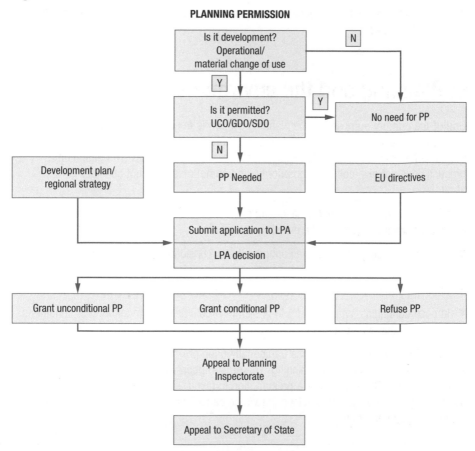

It is worth noting that the geographical area covered by an LPA, which is generally the county or district council (or unitary authority), may also overlap with an area covered by one of the following, which will take over the role that would ordinarily be played by the LPA.

- Joint Planning Board – Section 2 TCPA 1990 allows for the creation of a Joint Planning Board 'as the county planning authority for the areas or parts of the areas of any two or more county councils or as the district planning authority for the areas or parts of the areas of any two or more district councils'.

- National Park Authorities (s. 4A(2)(b) TCPA 1990).

- The Broads Authority (s. 5 TCPA 1990).

- Enterprise Zone Authorities 1980 (s. 6 TCPA 1990).

- Urban Development Corporation (s. 7 TCPA 1990).

- Housing Action Trusts (s. 8 TCPA 1990).

- Home and Communities Agency set up by s. 13 Housing and Regeneration Act 2008 (s. 8A TCPA 1990).

Planning and the environment

One of the primary purposes of the planning system is to control land use and development, and environmental considerations are only one aspect of this, albeit a crucial one. The RCEP 5th Report (in 1976) stated that 'The [planning] process does not give pollution top priority, and sometimes does not consider it at all.'

This is no longer necessarily the case, and planning has three broad areas where it can make a significant impact on the environment:

- Regional strategy – this gives an opportunity for considering matters at the policy-making level;

- Planning permission – the LPA can reject certain activities before they start; or

- Impose conditions, which will try to pre-empt problems – the monitoring of conditions also gives the LPA continued control over development.

Since 1985, government policy has traditionally been pro-development, and there has been a presumption to this effect in planning. The presumption was set out in Circular 14/85, which said that 'There is always a presumption in favour of allowing applications for development . . . unless the development would cause demonstrable harm to interests of acknowledged importance.'

In March 2012, the National Planning Policy Framework was published. This contained a **presumption in favour of sustainable development** which will have an impact on all planning decisions. Although this sounds quite dramatic, in reality the presumption simply formalises policy objectives that were already underpinning planning, and had been mooted since the 'Sustainable Communities: Delivering through Planning' White Paper published by the Office of the Deputy Prime Minister in 2002.

KEY DEFINITION: Presumption in favour of sustainable development (Para. 14, NPPR)

At the heart of the National Planning Policy Framework is a presumption in favour of sustainable development, which should be seen as a golden thread running through both plan-making and decision-making.

For plan-making this means that:

- local planning authorities should positively seek opportunities to meet the development needs of their area;
- Local Plans should meet objectively assessed needs, with sufficient flexibility to adapt to rapid change, unless:
  - any adverse impacts of doing so would significantly and demonstrably outweigh the benefits, when assessed against the policies in this Framework taken as a whole; or
  - specific policies in this Framework indicate development should be restricted.

For decision-making this means:

- approving development proposals that accord with the development plan without delay; and
- where the development plan is absent, silent or relevant policies are out-of-date, granting permission unless:
  - any adverse impacts of doing so would significantly and demonstrably outweigh the benefits, when assessed against the policies in this Framework taken as a whole; or
  - specific policies in this Framework indicate development should be restricted.

If sustainable development is embedded into the decision-making process of planning law, the question arises as to the extent to which the LPA can be concerned with environmental matters when deciding on an application.

KEY CASE

Gateshead Metropolitan Borough Council v *Secretary of State for The Environment* **[1995] Env LR 37**

Concerning: clinical waste incinerator – overlap between the functions of the local planning authority and HMIP

Facts

The LPA refused planning permission for a clinical waste incinerator as the applicant failed to supply sufficient information to demonstrate that the plant would operate without causing nuisance, including the possible release of noxious substances.

Legal principle

The SSE ruled that while the planning system must determine the location of facilities of this kind (taking account of provisions for the development and other material considerations), it is not the role of the planning system to duplicate controls given under the Environmental Protection Act 1990. It was considered at that time that it was for Her Majesty's Inspectorate of Pollution (now the Environment Agency) to deal with these matters.

The *Gateshead* case led to the introduction of PPG-23 ('Planning and Pollution Control'), which specified that the planning system should not duplicate controls which are the statutory responsibility of other bodies (e.g. the Environment Agency), and emphasised that the planning and pollution control systems are separate but complementary.

PPG-23 also stated that decisions on applications for developments which may give rise to pollution must be made in accordance with the development plan and EU Directives (unless material considerations indicate otherwise), and that LPAs should *consult* with relevant pollution control authorities but must assume that pollution control provisions will be properly applied and enforced.

There were criticisms of PPG-23, mainly based on the fact that it blurred the line between aspects of a scenario that should be dealt with by the LPAs and pollution control bodies. For example, the presence and impact of contamination, waste or toxic releases arising from a proposed development, and any relevant remediation work, can only be taken into account to the extent that they have land use implications.

A replacement PPS-23 ('Planning and Pollution Control') was produced in 2004 by the Office of the Deputy Prime Minister, and this too has been criticised for causing uncertainty.

 Make your answer stand out

This is an area of law which is undergoing changes, so look both at the criticisms of the previous law (for example, Martin (2009) and Lyness (2010)) and at the changes implemented by the National Planning Policy Framework and see whether the changes help to offset the criticisms.

The point that planners could, and should, assume that pollution control would be properly applied, which was reiterated in PPS-23, was called 'superficially attractive' and rejected by the court in *Hopkins Development Ltd* v *First Secretary of State* [2006] EWHC 2823 (Admin), although it has been argued (Thornton, 2008) that this different approach 'may be explained by the fact that the concern in question related to the less specialised issue of dust rather than air quality' (p. 610).

Material planning considerations

Despite all of the changes to legislation in recent years, the core of decision-making remains that consideration of applications must have regard to the development plan, and 'the determination shall be made in accordance with [it] unless material considerations indicate otherwise' (s. 38(6) PCPA 2004).

Legislation, whether it emanates from the EU or UK, is a material consideration although, since the development plan has to be drawn up in accordance with both, it is a moot point as to whether this is a valuable point.

In *Stringer* v *Minister of Housing and Local Government and Another* [1970] 1 WLR 1281, Cooke J set the tone for categorising what might amount to a material consideration by stating that 'any consideration which relates to the use and development of land is capable of being a planning consideration' (p. 1294).

The following are among those that have recently been held to be material considerations.

Material change	Case
Promoting social objectives	*R (on the application of Copeland)* v *Tower Hamlets LBC* [2010] EWHC 1845 (Admin)
The absence of a complaint from local residents	*Shahid* v *Secretary of State for Communities and Local Government* [2008] EWHC 2080 (Admin)

▓ Environmental impact assessment (EIA)

Many of the things which might amount to material considerations due to their impact on the environment can only be established by an accurate environmental assessment of the site, and the impacts which might be a result of the development.

The process of EIA was brought in via Directive 85/337/EEC on the assessment of the effects of certain public and private projects on the environment. That Directive has been amended subsequently (and is the subject of an ongoing consultation by the European Commission), which leaves the threshold criteria for whether EIA is required to the discretion of member states (Art. 4(2)(b)).

The UK implemented the Directive through the Town and Country Planning (Assessment of Environmental Effects) Regulations 1988; the most recent regulations are the Town and Country Planning (Environmental Impact Assessment) Regulations 2011 ('the 2011 EIA Regulations'). The Regulations split potential developments into Schedule 1 and Schedule 2.

> **☐ REVISION NOTE**
>
> There are strong links between environmental impact assessments and the old integrated pollution prevention and control (now environmental permitting) regime. Chapter 6 covers the permitting regime, and the basics of EIA should be kept in mind when answering questions on this topic.

Schedule 1 projects

Projects included under Schedule 1 are generally large-scale infrastructure projects, or those which have the potential to cause large-scale pollution. For these projects, an EIA is mandatory. It includes developments such as the following:

- crude-oil refineries;
- power stations (thermal of over 300mW, or nuclear);
- iron or steel foundries;
- lines for long-distance railway traffic and of airports with a basic runway length of 2,100 metres or more (Para. 7);
- ports.

Schedule 2 projects

Schedule 2 projects are those for which an EIA will be necessary if it is likely that there will be significant environmental effects due to the size, nature or location of the project. These are listed by broad industrial sector, and regulation 2, Schedule 2 contains an extensive table of 'descriptions of development and applicable thresholds and criteria' for deciding whether a project is classified as a Schedule 2 project.

Schedule 3 sets out a non-exhaustive list of the criteria which are likely to be significant, and this is substantially unchanged since Government Circular 15/88 from 25 years earlier:

- the characteristics of the development (size, risk, etc.);
- the location of the development;
- the characteristics of the potential impact (extent, magnitude, duration, etc.)

Because of the lack of certainty in the UK, any time prior to making formal application, an applicant may seek an opinion from the LPA whether a development falls into either Schedule 1 or 2, or neither. Figure 5.2 is a simplified pictorial representation of the procedure for submitting an EIA.

Figure 5.2

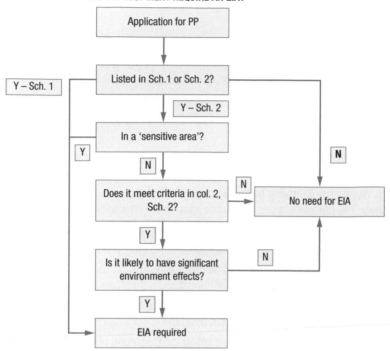

DOES DEVELOPMENT REQUIRE AN EIA?

For all projects that require an EIA to be carried out, an Environmental Statement (ES) will also be needed: without it the application will be treated as though a screening opinion has been sought from the local authority (reg. 7 of the 2011 EIA Regulations).

There is no set form for an ES but, regulation 2 of the 2011 EIA Regulations sets out that it must at least comply with Schedule 4 Part 1 and 2. Those Parts of the Schedule state that it must include descriptions of the following:

1. Description of the development, including in particular –

   (a) a description of the physical characteristics of the whole development and the land-use requirements during the construction and operational phases;

   (b) a description of the main characteristics of the production processes, for instance, nature and quantity of the materials used;

   (c) an estimate, by type and quantity, of expected residues and emissions (water, air and soil pollution, noise, vibration, light, heat, radiation, etc.) resulting from the operation of the proposed development.

2. An outline of the main alternatives studied by the applicant or appellant and an indication of the main reasons for the choice made, taking into account the environmental effects.

Criticisms of EIA

- Applies only to individual projects, rather than policies (NB: see strategic environmental assessment below, which applies to plans and programmes).
- Cumulative effects of projects are not necessarily assessed.
- The EIA only provides information to decision-makers and does not stipulate a course of action to be taken.
- Once the EIA is completed, there is no way to require further information or to highlight information needed to assist the LPA in its decision.
- Projects revealed as damaging by the EIA may still get the go-ahead on the basis of promises to mitigate. The process is a way to balance harm to the environment and benefits to society.
- The EIA is carried out by the developer, which might raise questions as to its objectivity.
- Often there is no non-technical summary, despite obligation on provision.
- The policy or presumption in favour of development means most parties will assume development will go ahead and look for mitigation, rather than challenging the decision.
- Objectors are merely 'planning objectors' – they have no participatory role (the *Greenpeace* case (see Chapter 4) did not open the floodgates).
- Situations where an EIA are needed are left to the discretion of the LPA (except for Schedule 1 projects where it is compulsory).
- Regarded (wrongly) as a bolt-on, rather than an integral, part of the planning process.
- Appeal procedure is to the SSE but courts are reluctant to interfere with the merits of any decision which required an EIA.

Strategic environmental assessment

Directive 2001/42/EC on the assessment of the effects of certain plans and programmes on the environment introduced the idea of a strategic environmental assessment. In the UK it was given effect by the Environmental Assessment of Plans and Programmes Regulations 2004. Bell, McGillivray and Pedersen lament the decision to drop 'policies' from the draft Directive, after strong opposition from some member states (2013: 488), and what remains is a system that applies to plans and programmes which are 'subject to preparation or adoption by an authority at national, regional or local level; or are prepared by an authority for adoption, through a legislative procedure by Parliament or Government; and, in either case, are required by legislative, regulatory or administrative provisions' (reg. 2).

In effect, the SEA procedure is substantially the same as the EIA procedure, but it relates to wider-scale activities, rather than specific, individual policies.

! Don't be tempted to . . .

Don't assume that just because an SEA has been carried out in relation to a particular programme that any projects occurring under the auspices of that programme are automatically excused the EIA process – there may be a requirement for both.

■ Putting it all together

Answer guidelines

See the problem question at the start of the chapter. A diagram illustrating how to structure your answer is available on the companion website.

Approaching the question

This question should be worked through, stage by stage, and any assumptions stated clearly, as they could have an impact on your answer. As the question is mute on the topic, you can assume that the site referred to is an ordinary industrial site in an ordinary town in England, and is not subject to any special planning regulations.

Important points to include

- Start with a discussion about the fundamentals of planning permission – what is its purpose, how has it developed, and so on.
- You could then move on to discuss the practical steps that an applicant would need to go through in order to apply for planning permission – include some discussion as to what counts as development (operational or material change of use) and also any types of permitted development.
- It is then time to move on to the *specifics* of the problem question. Take each aspect in turn – the factory, the canteen, the used-car lot, the fireworks storage – and link each aspect to the points you have made. Don't get sidetracked into issues around licensing the restaurant to sell alcohol, or issues around the storage of explosives. You must make sure that you 'advise James' rather than just discussing the topic in an essay-style answer. ▶

Make your answer stand out

The question has some points that are not clear, but most of these you can deal with as they occur. One contentious issue is that of the floodlighting. A discussion as to whether light pollution is subject to planning would impress the examiners. Morgan Taylor (2006) makes the point that some forms of external lighting is covered by the statutory nuisance provisions of the Clean Neighbourhoods and Environment Act 2005, and that Defra states that: 'The statutory nuisance regime is not an appropriate tool with which to address light pollution per se.'

READ TO IMPRESS

Bell, S., McGillivray, D. and Pedersen, O. (2013) *Environmental Law*, 8th Edn. Oxford: Oxford University Press

DCLG (2010) *Major Infrastructure Planning Reform: work plan*, London: Department for Communities and Local Government

DCLG (2011) *What We Are Doing: planning and the environment*, Department for Communities and Local Government, www.communities.gov.uk/planningandbuilding/planningenvironment/

Duxbury, R. (2006) *Telling & Duxbury's Planning Law and Procedure*, 13th Edn. Oxford: Oxford University Press

Humphreys, R. (2011) Material change in use: What's character got to do with it? *JPL* 3, 229–40

Lyness, S. (2010) Air quality: legal and policy issues, *Env. Law* 56, 6–20

Martin, J. (2009) Yet another fine mess, *EG* 0918, 76–8

McEldowney, P. and McEldowney, S. (2010) *Environmental Law*, Harlow: Longman

Taylor, M. (2006) Light pollution now subject to the criminal law of statutory nuisance, Campaign for Dark Skies, www.britastro.org/dark-skies/cleanact.html?10

Thornton, J. (2008) 'Mind the gap': a note on the boundaries between environmental and planning law, *JPL* 5, 609–14

www.pearsoned.co.uk/lawexpress

 Go online to access more revision support including quizzes to test your knowledge, sample questions with answer guidelines, podcasts you can download, and more!

Environmental permitting

6

Revision checklist

Essential points you should know:

☐ How the environmental permitting system developed

☐ The EU system of integrated pollution prevention and control

☐ Which activities are covered by an environmental permit

☐ How BAT works

☐ How the 2010 Permitting Regulations work

☐ The scope for public participation in environmental permitting

■ Topic map

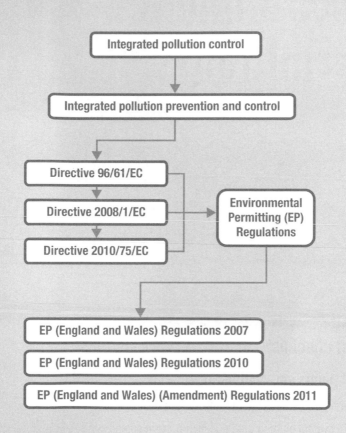

Integrated pollution control

↓

Integrated pollution prevention and control

Directive 96/61/EC

Directive 2008/1/EC

Directive 2010/75/EC

Environmental Permitting (EP) Regulations

EP (England and Wales) Regulations 2007

EP (England and Wales) Regulations 2010

EP (England and Wales) (Amendment) Regulations 2011

A printable version of this topic map is available from **www.pearsoned.co.uk/lawexpress**

■ Introduction

Environmental permitting may appear to be a new area of law, but in fact it builds upon a complex background which you must know in order to understand how it operates today.

No discussion about environmental permitting can hope to be complete without coverage of the background to the system. This is particularly true since permits issued under the IPPC system will remain valid until they need to be renewed. Back in 1976 the Royal Commission on Environmental Pollution (RCEP) 5th Report 'Air Pollution Control: An Integrated Approach' stated that:

> Reduction of emissions into the atmosphere can lead to an increase in [disposal] on land or into water. If the optimum environmental solutions are to be found, the controlling authority must be able to look comprehensively to all forms of pollution arising from industrial processes where different control problems exist (RCEP, 1976).

The RCEP also suggested the creation of a single regulatory agency, which led to Her Majesty's Inspectorate of Pollution (HMIP) in 1987. The current environmental permitting regime extends only to England and Wales, and the separate parallel regimes that exist in Scotland and Northern Ireland will not be covered.

📖 REVISION NOTE

The environmental permitting regulations also have a significant impact on the water pollution regime (see Chapter 8 on water pollution). There are also strong links between environmental permitting and environmental impact assessment (which was covered in Chapter 5 on planning). You should also consider the provision relating to waste (see Chapter 9 on waste management).

Having identified the inevitability that commercial pressures would drive some polluters to change the format of their pollution, rather than reduce it, the RCEP 5th Report also suggested the idea of the 'Best Practicable Environmental Option' (BPEO) as a replacement for the then current 'Best Practicable Means' approach. The RCEP returned to the idea of the BPEO in its 11th Report (Managing Waste: The Duty of Care) and defined it as:

> the option that provides the most benefit or the least damage to the environment as a whole, at acceptable cost, in the long term as well as in the short term (RCEP, 1985).

ASSESSMENT ADVICE

Since the current environmental permitting regulations are only starting to come into force now, there is no specific case law as yet. However, the regulations build on existing legislation, so there is a good quantity of case law relating to the aspects of IPPC that have been carried over. This area could be assessed equally by a problem, or essay question, and for answers to both types of question the key is to be absolutely clear that you demonstrate your awareness of the recent developments.

Sample question

Could you answer this question? Below is a typical essay question that could arise on this topic. Guidelines on answering the question are included at the end of this chapter, whilst a sample problem question and guidance on tackling it can be found on the companion website.

ESSAY QUESTION

'While some progress has been made, various opportunities to legislate for more integrated, harmonised and ambitious technology standards were missed in the reform of the EU regime of integrated pollution prevention and control.' (Lange, 2011: 199)

Critically assess the extent to which Directive 2010/75/EU reflects the established pattern of gradual change in the area of IPPC.

Integrated Pollution Prevention and Control (IPPC)

The integrated pollution prevention and control system was introduced by Directive 96/61/EC (concerning integrated pollution prevention and control) which gave member states until 1999 to implement a system of IPPC.

The system built on the existing IPC system, and any installations which had existing IPC licences were given until 2007 when they had to be brought in to the new system. This time lag reflects the length of some of the IPC licences that were granted.

The addition of 'prevention' to the scope of IPPC gave the Directive a much broader range of influence, and up to three times as many projects were included compared to the previous system.

The Directive set out to 'prevent or, where that is not practicable, to reduce emissions in the air, water and land . . . in order to achieve a high level of protection of the environment taken as a whole' (Art. 1), but makes it clear that this is 'without prejudice' to the EIA Directive (85/337/EEC).

Annex I covered (in great detail) the industries and the threshold values that would lead to an installation coming within the remit of the Directive. For these plants, the operators needed to obtain a permit both for new and existing installations from (in England and Wales) the Environment Agency. The Agency had the power to set conditions to the granting of a permit, provided these conditions complied with the basic principles and the environmental quality standards of the Community.

Annex III gave an indicative list of main polluting substances that needed to be taken into account when fixing emission standards for a permit.

In the UK, IPPC was introduced (late) by the Pollution Prevention and Control Act 1999 and the Pollution Prevention and Control (England and Wales) Regulations 2000.

The Directive was repealed and replaced by Directive 2008/1/EC concerning integrated pollution prevention and control, which brought together the many amendments that had been made.

Following a review of the IPPC Directive by the European Commission in 2007, which found that the Directive provided a firm basis for future developments but was generally too burdensome and ineffective, a proposal for a Directive on Industrial Emissions was adopted, which would provide a single, clear and coherent legislative instrument.

The Directive saw the light of day as Directive 2010/75/EU on industrial emissions (integrated pollution prevention and control) (sometimes referred to as the IE(IPPC) Directive) and recast seven existing Directives into a single entity. The seven Directives were the following:

- Directive 78/176/EEC on waste from the titanium dioxide industry;
- Directive 82/883/EEC on procedures for the surveillance and monitoring of environments concerned by waste from the titanium dioxide industry;
- Directive 92/112/EEC on procedures for harmonising the programmes for the reduction and eventual elimination of pollution caused by waste from the titanium dioxide industry;
- Directive 99/13/EC on the limitation of emissions of volatile organic compounds due to the use of organic solvents in certain activities and installations;
- Directive 2000/76/EC on the incineration of waste;
- Directive 2001/80/EC on the limitation of emissions of certain pollutants into the air from large combustion plants; and
- Directive 2008/1/EC concerning integrated pollution prevention and control.

The new Directive is not fully in force yet, and there are various deadlines for transposition into national law set out in Article 80, the earliest of which was January 2013. This was achieved in England and Wales by the Environmental Permitting (England and Wales) (Amendment) Regulations 2013.

> **✎ EXAM TIP**
>
> Make sure you are aware of the transposition deadlines and the dates that the various provisions come into effect – particularly if you are faced with a problem question set around a particular date.

The range of activities covered by the IPPC regime is quite broad, and includes (in Annex 1 of the 2010 Directive):

- Energy industries
- Production and processing of metals
- Mineral industry
- Chemical industry, and
- Waste management.

Each of these is subsequently split into a number of sub-categories, and there is also a sizeable list of activities in the 'other' category, ranging from cardboard production to the intensive rearing of pigs. One of the key elements which helps to determine whether an activity comes within the IPPC regime is that of scale, and within the general categories are provisions as to the scale of the operation. For example, s. 1.1 of Annex 1 provides for the inclusion of 'Combustion of fuels in installations with a total rated thermal input of 50 MW or more' as being within the remit of the Directive.

Article 11 sets out the eight basic principles with which the operators of all installations covered by the Directive would have to comply:

- all the appropriate preventive measures are taken against pollution;
- the best available techniques (BAT) are applied;
- no significant pollution is caused;
- the generation of waste is prevented in accordance with the Waste Framework Directive (Directive 2008/98/EC);
- if waste is generated, it is reused, recycled, recovered or, where that is technically and economically impossible, it is disposed of while avoiding or reducing any impact on the environment;
- energy is used efficiently;
- the necessary measures are taken to prevent accidents and limit their consequences;
- the necessary measures are taken upon definitive cessation of activities to avoid any risk of pollution and return the site of operation to the satisfactory state defined in accordance with Article 22.

The idea of remediating the site after use was not part of the original IPC process, and marks the beginnings of a more strategic approach. Article 22 expands on the post-closure site restoration, which is to be calculated against a baseline report produced 'before starting operation of an installation or before a permit for an installation is updated for the first time after 7 January 2013' (Art. 22(2)).

> **✎ EXAM TIP**
>
> You can discuss in an exam whether post-closure restoration of a site is a useful addition to pollution control, given both the potential time scales of some industrial operations, and the fact that a baseline study might not be completed until 2014.

Best available technique (BAT)

The 'best available technique' standard mentioned both in Directive 2008/1/EC and Directive 2010/75/EU is defined in Article 2(11) of the latter.

> **KEY DEFINITION: Best available technique (Article 2(11) Directive 2010/75/EU)**
>
> Best: most effective in achieving high level of protection of the environment as a whole.
>
> Techniques: both the technology used and the way in which the installation is designed, built, maintained, operated and decommissioned.
>
> Available: techniques developed on scale allowing implementation in relevant industrial sector under economically and technically viable conditions, taking into consideration costs/advantages as long as they are reasonably accessible to the operator.

Further guidance as to specific ideas that could be considered is included in Directive 2010/75/EU Annex III (Criteria for determining BAT), but it is clear to see that the regime was attempting to balance precaution and prevention with costs and benefits.

Article 11 of the 2010 Directive encourages the exchange of information between member states in relation to BAT, in order to promote harmonisation of standards across the EU. These BAT reference documents (or BREF documents), which are prepared by a combination of industry and NGOs, were included in the old regimes, but are made stronger in the 2010 Directive, where Articles 14 and 15 set out that the BREF documents should be the reference point used by member states.

There are various other bodies which are instrumental in the elaboration of BREFs, and these include DG Environment; the International Exchange Group (IEG); the International Exchange Forum (IEF); the IPPC Bureau; and the Technical Working Groups (TWGs).

McEldowney and McEldowney argue that BAT is one of the areas where the precautionary principle is 'embedded into general principles' (2011: 185) of law, and that this in turn is a good example of the collaboration between the law and science. They also point out that 'Collaboration between Environmental Lawyers and scientists is essential in the development of sustainable solutions to environmental problems' (2011: 169) and this illustrates the importance of interdisciplinarity that was mentioned in Chapter 3. Much as it is a function of the realm of science and technology to decide what is the current 'best', and it is down to economics to decide on the level of 'availability', it is still down to the law to rule on what is the BAT via individual case law.

The Environmental Permitting Regulations 2007

Under regulation 8 of the Pollution Prevention and Control (England and Wales) Regulations 2000, permits for IPPC were granted as follows:

- Part A(1) permits, for the most potentially polluting activities were granted by the EA.
- Part A(2) and Part B permits were granted by the 'local authority in whose area the installation is (or will be) situated'.

Part A(1) and (2) and Part B permits applied equally to fixed installations and mobile plant. As with the Directive, whether an activity came within Part A(1), A(2) or B depended on output. For example:

- A(1): Refining gas likely to involve the use of 1kt or more of gas in any 12-month period;
- A(2): Refining gas involving the use of less than 1kt of gas in any 12-month period; and
- B: Odorising natural gas (s. 1.2, Sch. 1).

The 2000 Regulations were repealed in 2007 by the Environmental Permitting (England and Wales) Regulations 2007 ('the 2007 Permitting Regulations'), which integrated the existing regimes covering waste management licensing and IPPC. The intention of these new regulations was to reduce the administrative burden on industry and regulators without compromising the environmental and human health standards previously delivered by these separate regimes.

The Regulations made no changes as to who was the regulator, what was regulated, or the standards that had to be met, but did streamline the system in relation to:

- who needs a permit or to register an exemption;
- how to apply for, vary, transfer, surrender and enforce against a permit; and
- the delivery through permitting of national policy and 11 European Directives on environmental protection.

The 11 Directives referred to are:

- Directive 87/217/EEC on the prevention and reduction of environmental pollution by asbestos;

- Directive 92/112/EEC on the reduction and eventual elimination of pollution from the titanium dioxide industry;

- Directive 94/64/EC on the control of volatile organic compound (VOC) emissions from petrol storage and distribution;

- Directive 2008/1/EC on integrated pollution prevention and control;*

- Directive 99/13/EC on the limitation of emissions of VOC due to the use of organic solvents;*

- Directive 99/31/EC on the landfill of waste;

- Directive 2000/53/EC on end-of-life vehicles;

- Directive 2000/76/EC on the incineration of waste;*

- Directive 2001/80/EC on the limitation of emissions of certain pollutants into air from large combustion plants;*

- Directive 2002/96/EC on waste electrical and electronic equipment; and

- Directive 2006/12/EC on waste management.

Four of these Directives (marked with an asterisk) are among the seven that were subsequently recast by the IE(IPPC) Directive, and the rest remain extant.

! Don't be tempted to . . .

Don't make the mistake of thinking that the environmental permitting regime extends beyond the UK – the EU regime of IPPC under the IE(IPPC) Directive remains unchanged. Similarly, remember that the various Environmental Permitting Regulations only extend to England and Wales.

For most of the Directives, all that the Permitting Regulations serve to do is restate the whole of the regime (or at least the main operating provisions) into the new system. Bell, McGillivray and Pedersen (2013: 501) say of the 2007 Permitting regime:

> This 'no change, but new rules' system operates by providing a single procedural framework that provides a broad outline for making applications and granting permits, as well as for monitoring and enforcement.

> This is coupled with a general duty upon regulators to 'exercise . . . relevant functions so as to achieve compliance with' the specified Directives.

> These relevant functions include determining permit applications, setting conditions, and enforcement against breach including variation and revocation.

It is only 'regulated facilities' that require a permit under the 2007 Permitting Regulations, and Article 8 sets out what classes as such a facility. The largest category is 'installations' and, in this regard, the activities covered under the 2007 Permitting Regulations were more or less the same as under IPPC – Part A(1), Part A(2) and Part B:

- Energy activities
- Mineral industries
- The chemical industry
- Waste operations
- Other activities
- SED (Solvent Emissions Directive 99/13/EC) Activities (Part 2, Sch. 1).

The main additional aspect is 'waste operations'.

□ REVISION NOTE

The waste operations aspects of the permitting regime are also discussed in Chapter 9 on waste management.

The Environmental Permitting Regulations 2010

The Environmental Permitting (England and Wales) Regulations 2010 ('the 2010 Permitting Regulations') widened the existing streamlined environmental permitting and compliance system in England and Wales by integrating existing permitting regimes covering water discharge consenting, groundwater authorisations, radioactive substances regulation authorisations and the outcomes of the Waste Exemptions Order Review into the permitting system.

They also bring Directive 2006/21/EC (on the management of waste from the extractive industries) and the permitting parts of Directive 2006/66/EC (on batteries and accumulators and waste batteries and accumulators) into the permitting system.

The 2010 Permitting Regulations further reduce the administrative burden of regulation on industry and regulators without compromising the environmental and human health standards previously delivered by the separate regimes, and create an extended permitting and compliance system that brings increased clarity and certainty for everyone on how the regulations protect the environment.

As with the 2007 Permitting Regulations, the 'regulated facilities' are covered in regulation 8, set out below. While it is important to know which types of facility are covered by the new regulations, they are set out in quite broad terms.

KEY STATUTE

The Environmental Permitting (England and Wales) Regulations 2010/675

8. – Interpretation: regulated facility and class of regulated facility

(1) In these Regulations, 'regulated facility' means any of the following –

   (i)   an installation,

   (ii) mobile plant,

   (iii) a waste operation,

   (iv) a mining waste operation,

   (v) a radioactive substances activity,

   (vi) a water discharge activity,

   (vii) a groundwater activity.

(2) But the following are not regulated facilities –

   (i)   an exempt facility,

   (ii) an excluded waste operation,

   (iii) the disposal or recovery of household waste from a domestic property within the curtilage of that property by a person other than an establishment or undertaking.

(3) . . .

(4) A regulated facility of any of the following classes may be carried on as part of the operation of a regulated facility of another class –

   (i)   waste operation;

   (ii) mining waste operation;

   (iii) water discharge activity;

   (iv) groundwater activity.

The details of what a permit must contain are set out in Regulation 14 of the 2010 Permitting Regulations and build on the required content for IPC and IPPC authorisations of the past.

KEY CASE

Ardley Against Incineration v *Secretary of State for Communities and Local Government* [2011] EWHC 2230 (Admin)

Concerning: direct effect; directives; environmental permits; planning permission; waste

Facts

Planning permission was granted by the Secretary of State, on the recommendation of the Planning Inspector, for an Energy from Waste plant. The application had ▶

previously been rejected by the local authority in 2009. The 2010 Permitting Regulations referred to Article 4 of Directive 2006/12/EC, which had been replaced by Article 13 of Directive 2008/98/EC, which had not yet been transposed into national law. AAI sought judicial review of the decision.

Legal principle

Held that the legality of the decision by the Secretary of State was unassailable, and that 'The only question, therefore, is whether, in reaching that decision, the Secretary of State erred' (Howell, para. 80). It was further held that the Secretary of State had not erred, and the application for Judicial Review was dismissed.

Public participation

Schedule 5 to the 2010 Permitting Regulations set out, inter alia, the provisions for public involvement in the permitting regime. The specifics are set out in several places, and it is worth noting the requirements.

Public participation/Consultation under the 2010 Permitting Regulations

Regulation	Requirement
26. Preparation and revision of standard rules	(2) ... the authority must consult – (a) such persons as it considers are representative of the interests of communities likely to be affected by, or persons operating, the regulated facilities described in the rules; and (b) such other persons as it considers are likely to be affected by or have an interest in the rules
29. Revocation of standard rules	Before revoking standard rules, the authority must consult the persons referred to in regulation 26(2)
59. Environment Agency: public participation statement	(1) The Agency must prepare and publish a statement of its policies for complying with its public participation duties [the duty is that in Regs. 26 & 29, and Paras. 6 & 8 of Sch. 5]

Regulation	Requirement
Schedule 5	
6.– Public participation in relation to certain applications	(1) [. . .], if this paragraph applies the regulator must, within the consultation communication period – (a) take the steps it considers appropriate to inform the public consultees of the application and the place and times its public register can be inspected free of charge; (b) invite the public consultees to make representations on the application; and (c) specify to the public consultees the address to which and the period within which representations are to be made
8.– Public participation in relation to regulator-initiated variations	(1) If this paragraph applies, the regulator must notify the operator – (a) that the public participation procedures in sub-paragraph (2) apply; (b) of the variation it proposes to the environmental permit; and (c) of any fee prescribed [. . .] (2) The regulator must – (a) take the steps it considers appropriate to inform the public consultees of the proposed variation; (b) invite the operator and the public consultees to make representations on the proposed variation; and (c) specify to the operator and the public consultees the address to which and the period within which representations are to be made

These classes of person to be consulted then are those who the 'rule-making authority' (regs. 26 and 29) or 'regulator' (Sch. 5) considers to be 'interested parties'. In Scotland, as Kirk and Blackstock point out, the equivalent regulations 'provide an opportunity for any person to comment' (2011: 105). This has clear links to Otton J's judgment in the *Greenpeace* case (*R* v *HM Inspectorate of Pollution, ex parte Greenpeace (No. 2)* [1994] Env LR 76) and the widening of *locus standi* to include pressure groups.

Make your answer stand out

Kirk and Blackstock (2011) discuss the development of public participation in environmental decision-making, and the changes that the 2010 Permitting Regulations have made in this area. A discussion of the impact of public participation, balanced with some of the points raised by Gunningham (2011) about wider governance issues in environmental enforcement will be sure to impress an examiner. You could also make mention of the Åarhus Convention and the Directives on access to environmental information (see Chapter 3 on sources and concepts of environmental law).

■ The Environmental Permitting Regulations 2011

In the autumn of 2011, the Environmental Permitting (England and Wales) (Amendment) Regulations 2011 came into force. These made some changes to the 2010 Permitting Regulations, but only in relation to radioactive substances and procedures. As the explanatory memorandum to the regulations (p. 1) explains, this was done:

> in order to provide a more modern, transparent and user-friendly system for the regulation of radioactive substances which present a very low risk to people and the environment, while at the same time maintaining the necessary level of protection.

The 2011 Regulations also take into account changes that have been made to Directive 2008/1/EC and the Water Framework Directive 2000/60/EC (see Chapter 8 on water pollution) by Directive 2009/31/EC on the geological storage of carbon dioxide (the 'Carbon Capture and Storage', or 'CCS' Directive).

■ Putting it all together

Answer guidelines

See the essay question at the start of the chapter.

Approaching the question

This is clearly an essay question that is asking you to take a longitudinal look at the IPPC regime. If it is being done as a piece of coursework, then naturally your first action will be to read the article from which the question was taken, though this will of course not be possible in exam conditions. You should start off with a brief background to the system, and signal the key changes that have been made by the various pieces of EU legislation. Once you have established the areas where you want to focus your discussion, you can move into the finer detail.

Important points to include

- Having identified the areas of change on which you want to base your answer, bring in any opportunities that were missed. For example, should the reliance on the BREF documents have been made stronger by the 2010 Directive? Has the importance of the economic aspect to the old BATNEEC and current BAT standards been overemphasised? This will give you a good opportunity to get to the underlying arguments behind IPPC as a way of controlling pollution.

- You could develop your arguments further by using the environmental permitting regime in England and Wales as an example of wider and deeper integration, and assess the relative success or otherwise of these moves. Bear in mind, of course, that the permitting regime is still relatively new, and may not have developed the richness that it will later exhibit.

 Make your answer stand out

One area where there is considerable room for discussion is that of public participation in environmental permitting. As we have seen, Kirk and Blackstock (2011) highlight the provisions between the 2010 Permitting Regulations, and you could consider the extent to which these fulfil the spirit of state obligations under the Åarhus Convention and Directive 2003/35/EC (the Public Participation Directive). This can be brought in as an opportunity to integrate decision-makers in the process.

READ TO IMPRESS

Bell, S., McGillivray, D. and Pedersen, O. (2013) *Environmental Law*, 8th Edn. Oxford: Oxford University Press

Gunningham, N. (2011) Enforcing environmental regulation, *J. Env. L.* 23(2), 169–201

Kirk, E.A. and Blackstock, K.L. (2011) Enhanced decision making: balancing public participation against 'better regulation' in British environmental permitting regimes, *J. Env. L.* 23(1), 97–116

Lange, B. (2011) Legislative comment: the EU directive on industrial emissions: squaring the circle of integrated, harmonised and ambitious technology standards? *Env. L. Rev.* 13(3), 199–204

McEldowney, J. and McEldowney, S. (2011) Science and environmental law: collaboration across the double helix, *Env. L. Rev.* 13(3), 169–98

RCEP (1976) *Air Pollution: An Integrated Approach*, Royal Commission for Environmental Pollution, 6th Report, London: HMSO

RCEP (1985) *Managing Waste: The Duty of Care*, 11th Report, London: HMSO

www.pearsoned.co.uk/lawexpress

 Go online to access more revision support including quizzes to test your knowledge, sample questions with answer guidelines, podcasts you can download, and more!

Air pollution

7

Revision checklist

Essential points you should know:

- [ ] How acid rain happens, and how international/EU policy is tackling it
- [ ] What ozone layer depletion is, and how international/EU policy is tackling it
- [ ] The causes (and cures) of climate change
- [ ] What UK policy and legislation are doing to tackle low-level air pollution

■ Topic map

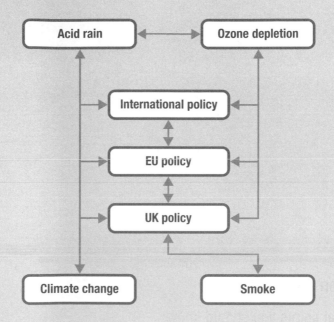

A printable version of this topic map is available from **www.pearsoned.co.uk/lawexpress**

◼ Introduction

Air pollution is likely to come up in one way or another in many environmental law exams. It is the most mobile of all forms of pollution and thus has the greatest potential to cause harm over a wide area.

This has meant that it is one of the most difficult types of pollution to control, for the effects of the pollution may be felt a long distance away from the source, possibly in a different country or even continent. If the huge topic of climate change is included within the broad range of air pollution, then clearly it is a problem which will have enormous effects and impacts for the foreseeable future. This chapter covers acid rain, ozone layer depletion and climate change, all of which have transboundary effects (and two are among what French calls the 'big three' of the global environment (2009: 271)), and then looks at how each has been dealt with by international and EU law. The section at the end of the chapter is limited to the UK, and is tied in with overall UK policy and legislation on air pollution.

As with all areas of environmental policy, air pollution controls are subject to overall government policy and, to that end, there will always be compromises between environmental protection and economic growth.

ASSESSMENT ADVICE

This topic area will generally be assessed through essay-type questions, either about the efficacy of a particular measure, or the impact of a particular problem. Remember the inherently transboundary impact of almost all airborne pollutants.

◼ Sample question

Could you answer this question? Below is a typical essay question that could arise on this topic. Guidelines on answering the question are included at the end of this chapter, whilst a sample problem question and guidance on tackling it can be found on the companion website.

ESSAY QUESTION

Atmospheric pollution has an adverse effect on both human health and the environment. Critically assess the measures being implemented to tackle atmospheric pollution.

Acid rain

Acid rain is problematic because it can lead to the pollution of rivers, lakes, forests and the built environment. As well as the environmental cost that ensues from this pollution, there is also an economic cost, especially for regions which rely heavily on forestry or aquaculture. The best-known example of this is the 'forest death' which afflicted Scandinavian countries in the 1970s and 1980s, where large swathes of pine forest were killed by acid rain.

The damage to the built environment, whilst it does not carry the same environmental problems as damage to the natural environment, is still costly to rectify. Cities such as Cambridge, where many of the historic buildings are of limestone construction, have found that the acidic nature of rain is reacting with the alkalinity of the buildings, and that they are literally dissolving – 'When sulfurous, sulfuric, and nitric acids in polluted air react with the calcite in marble and limestone, the calcite dissolves' (USGS, 1997).

Acid rain is almost entirely man-made, and is caused when chemicals emitted in industrial smoke react with water vapours in the atmosphere to form very weak acids, which eventually fall as rain, following the normal process of precipitation. In Northern Europe, for example, weather patterns tend to move from south west to north east, so pollutants emitted in the United Kingdom are likely to fall in Scandinavia and Russia. Where emission standards have been applied, this problem has largely been solved.

For example, sulphur dioxide (SO_2) is emitted in vehicle exhausts and from industrial premises. It rises into the sky and reacts with water vapour (H_2O) to form a weak solution of sulphurous acid (H_2SO_3). Similar reactions will occur with the release of nitrogen oxide (NO) to produce nitric acid (HNO_3), carbon monoxide (CO) and carbon dioxide (CO_2) to produce formic acid (H_2CO_2) and carbonic acid (H_2CO_3), and all similar pollutants.

Because the causes, impacts and range of acid rain are well understood, the solution to the problem is, at least conceptually, straightforward. Reducing the quantities of pollutants that are emitted by vehicles and industry will quite quickly reduce the amount of weak acid which is suspended in the air, and thus reduce the quantity, impact and cost (financial and environmental) of acid rain.

This can be achieved with 'bolt-on' or 'end-of-pipe' measures, such as the catalytic converters that are fitted to all new petrol cars, or 'stack scrubbers' on the chimneys of industrial premises, but these have their own environmental costs, and do not change the overall level of production of pollutants, just their release.

The better approach to the problem is for the introduction of cleaner and more efficient processes, which would mean that the pollutants are not being produced in the first place.

International policy

International policy in this area started with the UN Convention on **Long-Range Transboundary Air Pollution (LRTAP)**, signed in 1979 in Geneva. The Convention entered into force in 1983, after it had been ratified by 49 of the signatory states (which included the UK).

The requirements of the LRTAP were for the signatory states to limit and then reduce the levels of all air pollution, but particularly that which would have a transboundary impact. There was nothing particularly innovative about the LRTAP – indeed, the principle that a state should be liable for environmental damage it caused in a neighbouring state had been established three decades earlier in the Trail Smelter Arbitration (*United States* v *Canada* 3RIAA 1907 (1941)) – but what LRTAP did represent was a first step in the process of internationally agreed targets for the reduction of airborne pollutants.

KEY DEFINITION: Air pollution

(a) 'Air Pollution' means the introduction by man, directly or indirectly, of substances or energy into the air resulting in deleterious effects of such a nature as to endanger human health, harm living resources and ecosystems and material property and impair or interfere with amenities and other legitimate uses of the environment.

LRTAP, Article 1

KEY DEFINITION: Long-Range Transboundary Air Pollution (LRTAP)

(b) 'Long-range transboundary air pollution' means air pollution whose physical origin is situated wholly or in part within the area under the national jurisdiction of one State and which has adverse effects in the area under the jurisdiction of another State at such a distance that it is not generally possible to distinguish the contribution of individual emission sources or groups of sources.

LRTAP, Article 1

It has been argued (Winter, 2010: 15) that LRTAP 'established general obligations comparative to those of the FCCC' but that the targets imposed were far more draconian in their scope. There have been eight protocols to the LRTAP and, as the table shows, their impact is much more wide ranging than the FCCC (see below).

The eight protocols to the LRTAP

Protocol	Measure
Geneva (1984)	International cost-sharing of an air pollution monitoring programme. Entered into Force (EIF) 21/01/1988
Helsinki (1985)	Reduction of sulphur emissions by at least 30 per cent. EIF 02/09/1987
Sofia (1988)	Freeze emission levels of nitrogen oxides. EIF 14/02/1991
Geneva (1991)	Volatile organic compounds reduced by 30 per cent of 1990 levels by 1999. EIF 29/09/1997
Oslo (1994)	Further reduction of sulphur emissions. EIF 05/08/1998
Åarhus (1998)	Eliminate any discharges, emissions and losses of persistent organic pollutants. EIF 23/10/2003
Åarhus (1998)	Cadmium, lead, mercury should be reduced to below 1990 levels. EIF 29/12/2003
Gothenburg (1999)	2010 emission ceilings set for sulphur, NOx, VOCs and ammonia which should reduce Europe's sulphur emissions by at least 63 per cent, NOx emissions by 41 per cent, VOC emissions by 40 per cent and ammonia emissions by 17 per cent compared to 1990. EIF 17/05/2005

EU policy

The first piece of European legislation that relates to air pollution was Directive 70/220/EEC (on the approximation of the laws of the member states relating to measures to be taken against air pollution by gases from positive-ignition engines of motor vehicles). As can be seen, this is not legislation which relates to the environment per se, rather it sets out to ensure that the (then six) member states did not create laws that upset the 'level playing field' of European business.

☐ REVISION NOTE

Chapter 3 (on sources and concepts of environmental law) showed that, until the Paris Summit of 1973, the European Union did not consider environmental law to be within its remit. Also, look at the later *Commission* v *Denmark* Case 302/86 [1988] ECR 4607, by which stage the ECJ felt that the protection of the environment was 'one of the Community's essential objectives' and could justify restrictions on the free movement of goods.

If the first Directive relating to air pollution was in 1970, it was a further decade before the first Directive relating to air quality was produced. Directive 80/779/EEC (on air quality limit values and guide values for sulphur and suspended particulates) set out in its annexes the limit values ('which must not be exceeded') and guide values ('intended to serve as long-term precautions') for SO_2 and 'suspended particulates' – in other words: grit, smoke and dust.

The role of the 1980 Directive is currently fulfilled by Directive 2008/50/EC (on ambient air quality and cleaner air for Europe). This Directive covers everything which was previously covered by the Framework Directive on Air Quality (Directive 96/62/EC) and three of its four 'daughter directives' (Directive 99/30/EC (on limit values for SO_2, NO_2, particulate matter and lead); Directive 2000/69/EC (on limit values for benzene and CO_2); and Directive 2002/3/EC (on ozone)). The fourth daughter directive (Directive 2004/107/EC (on arsenic, cadmium, mercury, nickel and polycyclic aromatic hydrocarbons in ambient air)) has not yet been absorbed by the new Directive but, as Recital 4 makes clear, 'Once sufficient experience has been gained in relation to the implementation of Directive 2004/107/EC . . . consideration may be given to the possibility of merging its provisions with those of this Directive.'

A further aspect that marks out the new Directive is the inclusion of PM2.5 (fine particulate matter with a diameter of less than 2.5μm) which is identified as being 'responsible for significant negative impacts on human health' (Recital 11). Despite there being 'as yet no identifiable threshold below which PM2.5 would not pose a risk' (Recital 11), Annex XIV sets a limit value of 25μg/m^3 to be achieved by 2015, and 20μg/m^3 to be achieved by 2020. Article 15 requires member states to 'take all necessary measures not entailing disproportionate costs' to reach these values which Wilde points out is 'somewhat of a hostage to fortune . . . especially when the issue of economic recession is constantly in the background' (2010: 286–7).

The new directive works alongside Directive 2010/75/EC on industrial emissions, which imposes emission standards on industrial plants.

📖 REVISION NOTE

For questions relating to industrial emissions in England and Wales, you'll need to know about the Environmental Permitting Regulations (England and Wales) Regulations 2010. (See Chapter 6 on environmental permitting.)

■ Ozone layer depletion

The second area which has generated much transnational legislation and policy is that of the depletion of the ozone layer. Ozone (O_3) is a triatomic allotrope of oxygen, which is much less stable that the diatomic allotrope (O_2), and which plays a double role in relation to the environment. This is succinctly summarised by a 2003 publication of the US Environmental Protection Agency called *Ozone: Good up high, bad nearby.*

At low level (in the troposphere), ozone is caused by sunlight reacting with hydrocarbons emitted from exhausts, and oxides of nitrogen emitted from industry. Tropospheric ozone is a constituent part of smog, and brings with it all of the associated health risks. The Inter-Governmental Panel on Climate Change (IPCC) estimates that tropospheric ozone is also a greenhouse gas with about one-quarter of the warming effect of CO_2 but with the more problematic ability to extend 'the lifetimes of other greenhouse gases, such as CH_4.'

Although it can be dispersed over reasonable areas, it is generally not a transboundary problem, and national measures used to reduce emissions of hydrocarbons and oxides of nitrogen will lead to a reduction in this type of ozone.

High-level, or stratospheric, ozone exists in a fluctuating layer which effectively screens UV-B rays from the sun. A thinning of the ozone layer has been linked to increased risks of developing skin cancer in humans, and deleterious effects on plants and animals.

The depletion of the ozone layer is, even more so than acid rain, entirely caused by human activity. The use of CFCs (chlorofluorocarbons), H-CFCs (hydrochlorofluorocarbons) and halon in various industrial processes and as aerosol propellants means that there are inevitably some leaks and releases. These substances contain chlorine, bromine, nitric oxide and hydroxyl, which react with the ozone to break it down into oxygen, which does not have the same screening effects.

International policy

International law in this area stems from the 1985 Vienna Convention for the Protection of the Ozone Layer, which entered into force in September 1988, having been ratified by 20 countries (including the EU and UK).

The purpose of the Convention (Art. 2) is to take '. . . appropriate measures . . . to protect human health and the environment against adverse effects resulting or likely to result from human activities which modify/are likely to modify the Ozone Layer.'

At the time of the Convention, CFCs are only mentioned in Annex I as one of a number of substances that 'are thought to have the potential to modify the chemical and physical properties of the ozone layer' (ozone depleting substances, or ODS) and need monitoring (Art. 4(c) Annex I).

The scope and focus of the Vienna Convention was improved by the 1987 Montréal Protocol. This Protocol (which, you will note was signed before the Convention itself came into force) came into force in January 1989. It set out in its Annex a list of 'Controlled Substances' along with targets for reduction in consumption and production. The controlled substances were five types of CFC (Group I) and three types of halon (Group II). The Protocol also established three expert panels: the Scientific Assessment Panel (SAP), the Environmental Effects Assessment Panel (EEAP), and the Technology and Economic Assessment Panel (TEAP).

Both the Vienna Convention and the Montréal Protocol have been ratified by 196 states, and there have been four amendments to the Protocol which have made various changes and have been ratified by different numbers of parties.

The four amendments to the Montréal Protocol

Amendment (date)	Fundamental changes
London (1990)	Added Annex B Group 1 (10 types of CFC). Limits on consumption and production based on 1990 levels
	Added Annex B Group II (carbon tetrachloride). Limits on consumption and production based on 1990 levels. Target for 2000 is zero
	Added Annex B Group III (1,1,1, trichloroethane). Limits on consumption and production based on 1990 levels. Target for 2005 is zero
	Added Annex C Group I (34 types of H-CFC)
Copenhagen (1992)	Extended Annex C Group I to 40 H-CFCs
	Added Annex C Group II (34 types of HBFC (Hydrobromofluorocarbons)). States to reduce consumption to zero, and to ban import from and export to non-party states.
	Added Annex E Group I (methyl bromide). Limits on consumption and production (to pre-1990 levels)
Montréal (1997)	Added methyl bromide to ban on imports from/exports to non-signatory states
Beijing (1999)	Added Annex C Group III (bromochloromethane)
	Added Annex C Group I and Annex C Group II to ban on imports from/exports to non-signatory states

The impact of the Convention, its Protocol and Agreements was that production and consumption of ODS globally is almost zero, and has been falling for over 20 years. NASA satellites reveal that the greatest amount of ozone layer 'thinning' over Antarctica occurred in 2006, and that the measures in the treaty are having a gradual effect, but 'the Antarctic ozone hole is expected to continue for decades. Antarctic ozone abundances are projected to return to pre-1980 levels around 2060–2075' (WMO, 2010: xx).

EU policy

The Vienna Convention was approved by the EU on 31 October 1988 (*OJ L* 297, 31 October 1988: 8), although action on some of the substances contained in the Convention had already been taken. Council Decision 80/372/EEC, which built on a Council Resolution of

30 May 1978 (*OJ C* 133, 7 June 1978: 1), required member states to take all appropriate measures both to ensure that there was no growth in production capacity of CFC-11 and CFC-12 (Art. 1(1)) and also to reduce the use of CFC-11 and CFC-12 in aerosol cans by 30 per cent of 1976 levels by the end of 1981 (Art. (1)(2)).

Current EU law is set out in Regulation 1005/2009, which has imposed bans on some of the ODS in advance of what was required under the Vienna Convention. Annex I lists 'controlled substances' (which are effectively the same as Annexes A, B and C of the amended Protocol), and bans production (Art. 4), placing on the market and use (Art. 5), and 'Placing on the market of products and equipment containing or relying on controlled substances' (Art. 6), other than in very limited cases which meet the exemption criteria in Part III. There has been a minor amendment to the Regulations, set out in Regulation 744/2010, but this only relates to halons.

■ Climate change

Climate change (sometimes called 'global warming' or the 'enhanced greenhouse effect') is a problem which cannot be explored fully in a revision text such as this. For specific details on the science, politics and debates about climate change, you should look at, among others, Al Gore's *An Inconvenient Truth* but also Nigel Lawson's *An Appeal to Reason: A Cool Look at Global Warming*.

The basics of climate change are that changing weather patterns created by a warming atmosphere will lead to the following conditions:

- reduced crop yields (even if temperature is warmer earlier in the year, the nights will be just as long, flowers will be out of synch with pollinators, etc.);
- increased flooding (a 1m sea level rise will flood almost one-fifth of the land area of Bangladesh, for example);
- desertification;
- species extinction – some species are adaptable, others are quite sensitive – an average annual rise of 1 degree Celsius is sufficient to kill the balsam fir, for example;
- higher frequency 'extreme weather events' (Vellinga and van Verseveld, 2000).

Bell, McGillivray and Pedersen state, with masterful understatement, that 'addressing the problem of climate change has proved to be a much greater challenge than achieving consensus on the problem of ozone depletion' (2013: 543).

The core of the problem stems from the fact that, unlike acid rain or ozone layer depletion, the greenhouse effect is a natural phenomenon and indeed is what makes life on earth (as we know it) possible. Greenhouse gases (GHG – chiefly carbon dioxide, methane and ozone) trap some of the warmth from the sun in the atmosphere and raise the overall average temperature. Any dissent that remains hinges around the extent to which anthropocentric (i.e. human) emissions of these gases are impacting on the natural cycle of global warming and cooling.

The mechanics of reducing global GHG emissions are conceptually straightforward, but achieving consensus on implementation measures is, as Bell et al. say, a great challenge. Approaches include the following:

- planting more trees (this is effectively an end-of-pipe approach, since it relies on the natural absorption of CO_2 by trees, rather than changing the processes that emit the CO_2);

- harnessing methane as a power source;

- using alternative fuels in vehicles – electricity (centralises emissions to power stations), ethanol (no CO_2, but does produce carcinogenic formaldehyde) or others;

- renewable energy.

! Don't be tempted to . . .

Don't assume that even with widespread international agreement on the scientific background to climate change, there will be consensus as to how to tackle it. There is a clear divide between the approaches that tend to be favoured by developing nations (especially China, Brazil and India) and the approaches favoured in the West. Remember that this is a highly contentious political issue, as well as a legal one.

International policy

The main piece of international law in this area is, of course, the Framework Convention on Climate Change (FCCC) agreed at the UNCED in 1992. The FCCC was signed by 154 countries, and came into force in 1994, having been ratified by 50. The FCCC has (of January 2012) been ratified by 195 countries.

The text of the FCCC did not contain a great deal of detail, but included a commitment by states to implement national or regional measures with 'the aim of returning individually or jointly to their 1990 levels these anthropogenic emissions of carbon dioxide and other greenhouse gases' (Art. 4(2)(b)).

The real detail was added in 1997 by the Kyoto Protocol, Annex A of which set out the six GHG on which states were to focus the efforts, and Annex B listed the amounts that these should be reduced by when compared to 1990 levels. In the UK (and across the EU), this was an 8 per cent reduction.

- Carbon dioxide (CO_2)
- Methane (NH_4)

- Nitrous oxide (N_2O)
- Hydrofluorocarbons (HFCs)
- Perfluorocarbons (PFCs)
- Sulphur hexafluoride (SF_6).

The Protocol also put in place three market-based mechanisms to help countries meet their targets. They are **joint implementation (JI)**, **clean development mechanism (CDM)** and **emissions trading**.

KEY DEFINITION: Joint implementation (JI) (FCCC, 2011, Art. 6)

The equivalent to CDM, but both countries are developed.

KEY DEFINITION: Clean development mechanism (CDM) (FCCC, 2011, Art. 12)

Countries can offset their carbon reduction targets by implementing an emission-reduction project in developing countries.

KEY DEFINITION: Emissions trading (FCCC, 2011, Art. 17)

Countries with emission units to spare – emissions permitted them but not 'used' – can sell this excess capacity to countries that are over their targets. Carbon, for example, is now tracked and traded like any other commodity.

The most recent COP (Conference of the Parties) was in November 2012 in Doha, Qatar. The outcomes included a decision by Parties to extend the life of the Kyoto Protocol to 2020 (it had been due to expire in 2012) and to back the agreement by the previous COP in Durban, South Africa, to adopt a universal legal agreement on climate change as soon as possible, and no later than 2015.

The FCCC (2011) itself explains that 'while the Convention encouraged industrialised countries to stabilize GHG emissions, the Protocol commits them to do so'.

EU policy

As a signatory to the FCCC and the Kyoto Protocol, the EU is bound by the terms of both, and to reduce overall emissions by 8 per cent by 2012.

'Based on estimates for 2012 by the European Environment Agency, EU-15 emissions averaged 12.2% below base-year levels during the 2008-2012 period.' (DG CLIMA 2014).

In February 2010, the new Directorate-General for Climate Action (DG CLIMA) was formed. DG CLIMA controls the EU Emissions Trading System (EU ETS), which was implemented in 2005 under the auspices of the Kyoto Protocol via Directive 2003/87/EC.

Directive 2003/87/EC establishing a scheme for greenhouse gas emission allowance trading within the Community

Article 1
This Directive establishes a scheme for greenhouse gas emission allowance trading within the Community (hereinafter referred to as the 'Community scheme') in order to promote reductions of greenhouse gas emissions in a cost-effective and economically efficient manner.

. . .

Article 4
Member States shall ensure that, from 1 January 2005, no installation undertakes any activity listed in Annex I resulting in emissions specified in relation to that activity unless its operator holds a permit issued by a competent authority . . .

The EU ETS works by capping the total quantity of emissions permitted, and then allowing a trade to develop. 'The number of allowances is reduced over time so that total emissions fall. In 2020 emissions will be 21% lower than in 2005' (DG CLIMA, 2013).

Only certain industries are currently covered by the EU ETS, and these are listed in Annex I. Broadly speaking, the categories are energy activities, production and processing of ferrous metals, mineral industries and 'other', which covers pulp and paper production. It is also worth noting that, despite the all-encompassing title of the 'emissions' trading system, it does in fact currently just cover CO_2 emissions.

The legality of the provisions of the EU ETS were established by *Arcelor SA* v *European Parliament* Case T-16/04 [2010] Env LR D7, where a challenge to the Directive on the basis that it breached the community objective of freedom of establishment was rejected by the Court.

Directive 2008/101/EC (amending Directive 2003/87/EC so as to include aviation activities in the scheme for greenhouse gas emission allowance trading) added 'all flights which arrive at or depart from an aerodrome situated in the territory of a Member State to which the Treaty applies shall be included' in the EU ETS from 1 January 2012. A separate amendment, Directive 2009/29/EC, which introduced a new series of gradually reducing overall carbon limits, came into effect on 1 January 2013.

Make your answer stand out

As expected, the addition of air traffic to the ETS regime has been widely supported by environmental pressure groups (see www.transportenvironment.org, 2011) and criticised by airlines (see IATA, 2011). It was also subject to an unsuccessful action for judicial review and referral to the ECJ (see below). Impress the examiners by discussing the pros and cons of such an addition.

■ UK policy on air pollution

Section 80 of the Environment Act 1995 created a requirement on the Secretary of State to publish a National Air Quality Strategy (NAQS), which was to be modified from time to time as the need arose. The first NAQS was published in 1997, and the most recent in 2007 and, although the NAQS has no statutory force itself, the EA must have regard to it when it is exercising its pollution control powers.

The strategy has not been replaced, per se, but in March 2010 Defra published *Air Pollution: Action in a Changing Climate* which was 'intended to outline a wider vision for how we can link the two drivers for action [climate change and air pollution] more closely together' (Defra, 2010). Annex A of the document sets out the five key pollutants (PM2.5/PM10, nitrogen oxides, ozone (tropospheric), sulphur dioxide and ammonia) and provides an explanation of the health and environmental effects, but does not introduce or amend any targets. According to an Environmental Audit Committee report in November 2011, 'The UK is still not meeting EU limit values or UK objectives for PM10 particulate matter and NO_2 and is predicted by some to fail to meet targets for fine particulate matter (PM2.5)' (2011: 8).

The Air Quality (England) Regulations 2000 put into place binding targets for the maximum concentrations of seven pollutants, along with dates by which these targets needed to be achieved. These were the same deadlines as contained in the 2007 NAQS, as they were primarily EU deadlines. The 2000 Regulations were amended by the Air Quality (England) (Amendment) Regulations 2002 which simply changed the target for butadiene.

Emissions trading

The UK's foray into emissions trading started in 2002, with a voluntary system which participants could decide to engage in. As such, it was of limited success, and the scheme ended in 2006 (Dahlgreen, 2006). The EU ETS was introduced in the UK by the Greenhouse Gas Emissions Trading Scheme Regulations 2003 (replaced by the Greenhouse Gas Emissions Trading Scheme Regulations 2005). Also in 2005, the Greenhouse Gas Emissions

Trading Scheme (Amendment) and National Emissions Inventory Regulations 2005 made some procedural changes to the 2005 Regulations to add the JI/CDM provisions of Kyoto, but also added the provision for a National Emissions Inventory (Art. 10).

> **✎ EXAM TIP**
>
> Currently, the EU ETS is limited to Annex I industries. Consider whether, given the emissions that are generated from other industries, there is a need to extend the ETS system further.

The UK implemented Directive 2008/101/EC (above) with the Aviation Greenhouse Gas Emissions Trading Scheme Regulations 2009, which have subsequently been replaced by the Aviation Greenhouse Gas Emissions Trading Scheme Regulations 2010.

> **KEY CASE**
>
> *R (on the application of Air Transport Association of America Inc)* v *Secretary of State for Energy and Climate Change* [2010] EWCA 1554 (Admin); [2012] 2 CMLR 4
> *Concerning: airlines ETS; greenhouse gas emissions*
>
> **Facts**
>
> The Aviation Greenhouse Gas Emissions Trading Scheme Regulations 2009 were challenged, and the grounds of the challenge focused on the lawfulness of the European Directive 2008/101/EC underlying the Regulations. The case was referred to the ECJ for a preliminary ruling which 'could have [had] serious impact' (Barham and Cockrell, 2011).
>
> **Legal principle**
>
> The ECJ held that the Directive was valid, and that if an operator had chosen to operate a commercial air route arriving at or departing from an aerodrome situated in the territory of a Member State then the operator, because its aircraft was in the territory of that Member State, would be subject to the scheme (p. 162, para. 127)

Climate Change Act 2008

The CCA 2008 had two key aims and these were (Grekos, 2010: 454) '(1) to improve carbon management and help the transition towards a low carbon economy in the United Kingdom; and (2) to demonstrate strong UK leadership internationally'. The Act follows the lead of Kyoto and the EU ETS, but goes further into what McEldowney and McEldowney call 'a scoping exercise providing an arena for government policy to be developed' (2010: 336).

KEY STATUTE

Climate Change Act 2008

Part 1	Carbon Target and Budgeting
	Sets carbon budgets for 2050 and interim ones, along with baselines for emissions
Part 2	The Committee on Climate Change (CCC)
	Establishes the CCC, and gives it a range of powers and duties
Part 3	Trading Schemes
	Sets up ETS
Part 4	Impact of and adaption to Climate Change
	Provisions about reports from CCC and devolved administrations
Part 5	Other Provisions
	Including waste (repealed by the Localism Act 2011), renewable transport

---

■ Putting it all together

Answer guidelines

See the essay question at the start of the chapter.

Approaching the question

This is quite a broad question that potentially covers the whole range of different types of atmospheric pollution. Depending on the time and space you have available, you could restrict your answer to particular types of pollutants (e.g. particulate matter, ODS, GHG). This will naturally have an impact on the way you answer the question, as some are being tackled more effectively than others.

Important points to include

■ Whichever type of pollution you decide to focus on, start with outlining what measures have been implemented – this could be at an international, regional, national or local level.

- You can then move on to consider whether these measures have had any impact – this is also the section where you can discuss the assertion made in the first part of the question, and explore whether the measures you are looking at are (or should be) more concerned with protecting human health or protecting the environment. You can bring in areas covered in Chapter 1 on the philosophy of law if you have the opportunity.

- Once you have discussed the impact of your particular focus, you can draw together the criticisms of the process (and there will definitely be some) and use these to develop some suggestions as to improvements to the systems.

 Make your answer stand out

Areas such as ODS and acid rain are generally accepted, but there are contentious areas in relation to more or less everything to GHG emissions. You could discuss the inclusion of aviation (see above) or Winter's (2010) discussions about emissions trading systems.

READ TO IMPRESS

Barham, S. and Cockrell, C. (2011) ECJ decision on ETS could have serious impact, *LLID* 28 Jan, 7

Bell, S. McGillivray, D. and Pedersen, O. (2013) *Environmental Law*, 8th Edn. Oxford: Oxford University Press

Dahlgreen, J. (2006) Emissions trading in the UK, *Env. L. Rev.* 8(2), 134–43

Defra (2010) *Air Pollution: Action in a Changing Climate*, Department for Environment Food and Rural Affairs, Report PB13378, London: TSO

DG CLIMA (2013) *EU Emissions Trading Systems*, European Commission Directorate General for Climate Action, Brussels

DG-CLIMA (2014) *EU Greenhouse Gas Emissions and Targets*, European Commission Directorate General for Climate Action, Brussels

FCCC (2011) Kyoto Protocol, UN Framework Convention on Climate Change, http://unfccc.int/ kyoto_protocol/items/2830.php

French, D. (2009) Finding autonomy in international environmental law and governance, *J. Env. L.* 21(2), 255–89

Grekos, M. (2010) Climate Change Act 2008, *JPL* 4, 454–5

IATA (2011) CEO Brief, June 2011, Montréal: International Air Transport Association

McEldowney, P. and McEldowney, S. (2010) *Environmental Law*, Harlow: Longman

USGS (1997) How does acid precipitation affect marble and limestone buildings? *US Geological Survey*, http://pubs.usgs.gov/gip/acidrain/5.html

Vellinga, P. and van Verseveld, W. (2000) *Climate Change and Extreme Weather Events*, Gland: WWF

Wilde, M. (2010) The new directive on ambient air quality and cleaner air for Europe, *Env. L. Rev.* 12(4), 282–90

Winter, G. (2010) The climate is no commodity: taking stock of the emissions trading system, *J. Env. L.* 22(1), 1–25

WMO (2010) *WMO Antarctic Ozone Bulletin 2010*, Geneva: World Meteorological Organisation

www.pearsoned.co.uk/lawexpress

 Go online to access more revision support including quizzes to test your knowledge, sample questions with answer guidelines, podcasts you can download, and more!

Water pollution

8

Revision checklist

Essential points you should know:

- [ ] Ways of achieving and maintaining water quality (e.g. classification and setting standards and objectives)
- [ ] Consents
- [ ] Water pollution offences and defences
- [ ] How the Water Framework Directive and its daughter directives on Groundwater and Priority Substances work

■ Topic map

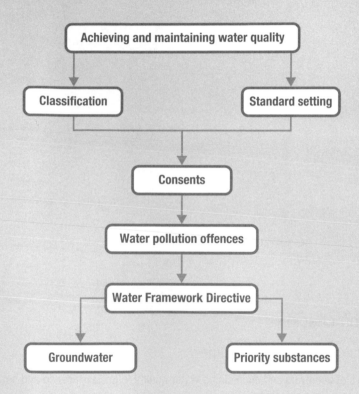

A printable version of this topic map is available from **www.pearsoned.co.uk/lawexpress**

■ Introduction

Water is essential to life and, as McEldowney and McEldowney rightly say, 'the need for healthy and drinkable water quality is likely to be at the centre of many conflicts in the world' (2010: 265).

In September 2010, *Nature* published a map showing the predicted possible extent of global water shortages by 2050 and indicating that 'nearly 80% of the world's population is exposed to high levels of threat to water security' (Vörösmarty et al., 2010).

Given these predictions, it is important to ensure that water quality is maintained and that pollution is kept to acceptable levels.

ASSESSMENT ADVICE

Water pollution could easily form the whole of an essay or problem question, or part of a wider question.

Essay questions

A common theme for essay questions would be to ask you to evaluate the impact of Directive 2000/60/EC ('the Water Framework Directive') on the pollution control regime in the EU. You should watch out for the implementation dates of the daughter directives.

Problem questions

Examples are:

What counts as controlled water for s. 85 Water Resources Act 1991?

Whether a series of events could be 'causing or knowingly permitting'.

■ Sample question

Could you answer this question? Below is a typical essay question that could arise on this topic. Guidelines on answering the question are included at the end of this chapter, whilst a sample problem question and guidance on tackling it can be found on the companion website.

■ Achieving and maintaining water quality

Water pollution comes from three main sources:

- specific outlets (pipelines, etc.);
- run-off/percolation from industrial plants or agricultural land (often called diffuse water pollution);
- accidental spillage.

There are minor differences in the way that the three different sources can be dealt with, and these will be explored as we progress.

The Royal Commission on Environmental Pollution separates the types of pollutant from these sources into three categories (RCEP, 1972: 29):

- untreated sewage (important because of volume);
- heavy metals and organochlorine compounds (important because of persistence);
- other pollutants.

In order to manage water quality, which will be affected by pollutants from all of the sources, and of all three categories, the Water Resources Act 1991 (WRA) sets out that it first needs to be classified (which can be done in a number of ways) (s. 82 WRA). Once classification has been made, then standards can be set as to the desired quality of the water (s. 83 WRA), and an enforcement system put into place to ensure that the standards are met (s. 84 WRA).

Classification

Prior to the WRA (ss. 82–84), water in the UK was classified according to the non-statutory guidance given by the National Water Council in 1970, which classified water primarily according to physical and chemical characteristics.

NWC River Quality Classification Scheme (RCEP, 1992: 31)

River class	Current potential uses
1A Good quality	High quality suitable for potable supply abstractions and for all other abstractions
1B Good quality	Less high quality . . . but usable for substantially the same purposes
2 Fair quality	Suitable for potable supply after advanced treatment
3 Poor quality	Polluted to an extent that fish are absent or only sporadically present. May be used for low grade industrial abstraction purposes. Considerable potential for further use if cleaned up
4 Bad quality	Grossly polluted and are likely to cause nuisance

This classification system is no longer used, but still 'provides a useful insight into the link between water quality and water usage' (Wolf and Stanley, 2010: 141).

The current system of classification is found in the WRA.

KEY STATUTE

Section 82(2) Water Resources Act 1991

(2) The criteria specified in regulations under this section in relation to any classification shall consist of one or more of the following, that is to say –

(a) general requirements as to the purposes for which the waters to which the classification is applied are to be suitable;

(b) specific requirements as to the substances that are to be present in or absent from the water and as to the concentrations of substances which are or are required to be present in the water;

(c) specific requirements as to other characteristics of those waters.

These provisions can be summarised as 'use', 'content' and 'other characteristics'.

Use

Under this criterion, water is classified according to the use for which it is suitable – in other words, drinking water, bathing water and water suitable for breeding shellfish are required to reach a different standard. Most of these standards are set at an EU level, for example the Surface Waters (Shellfish) (Classification) (Amendment) Regulations 2009 gave effect to Directive 2006/113/EC on the quality required of shellfish waters, and set out the standards required of water that is used for the production of shellfish.

Don't forget the relationship between the EU and the UK in relation to law-making powers. (See Chapter 3 on sources and concepts of environmental law.)

Content

The acceptable amount of certain dangerous substances in water, irrespective of use, is currently governed in England and Wales by the Surface Waters (Dangerous Substances) (Classification) Regulations 1998.

Elsewhere in the EU, Directive 2006/11/EC (on pollution caused by certain dangerous substances discharged into the aquatic environment of the Community) governs this area of regulation. The Directive sets up emission standards (see below) with regard to two lists of pollutants. List 1 contains substances that are 'selected mainly on the basis of their toxicity, persistence and bioaccumulation' and Article 3 requires that pollution by these substances be eliminated. List II contains substances that are less problematic, and which member states are required to reduce.

Other characteristics

In England and Wales, Schedule 1 to the Surface Waters (River Ecosystem) (Classification) Regulations 1994 sets out a series of classifications which govern the permitted oxygen, ammonia, copper and zinc content, pH level and hardness of all 'relevant watercourses' (s.104 WRA) regardless of their content or their prospective uses.

Setting standards and objectives

Once water has been classified, the next stage is to set out target standards and objectives that will lead to improvement in water quality. These standards are set in various directives, and it is important to remember that they are not static – as scientific knowledge changes, so will the permitted levels of some pollutants.

Generally, objectives are set according to either emission standards, environmental quality standards or, in some cases, a mixture of both. See Chapter 4 on enforcement of environmental law for a detailed discussion of these standards.

Emission standards

These are put in place on planned, point-specific types of pollutants. Remember that these sources are only one of the three types identified earlier in the chapter.

For example, regulation 58(2) of the Environmental Permitting (England and Wales) Regulations 2010 stipulates that at 'any time the Agency may give notice to the local authority specifying the emission limit values or the conditions it considers appropriate for preventing or reducing emissions into water from the installation or mobile plant'.

Environmental quality standards

Environmental quality standards (EQS) are also called target standards and, instead of looking at individual polluters, they concentrate on the receiving environment. In the wider context, the receiving environment could be a human, but in the context of this chapter, the receiving environment is usually a body of water.

The best example in this context is Directive 2008/105/EC on environmental quality standards in the field of water policy, which sets out, in Part A of Annex 1, a list of EQS relating to a number of different substances.

The Water Framework Directive (discussed later in the chapter) adopts a position which uses both ES and EQS in parallel.

■ Consents

Deliberate water pollution in England and Wales was initially controlled by the Environment Agency (see Chapter 4 on enforcement of environmental law) in three different ways:

■ the IPPC/environmental permitting regime (see Chapter 6);

■ issuing consents to discharge substances into controlled waters (s. 90A WRA);

■ issuing licences to abstract water (ss. 34–37 WRA).

> **□ REVISION NOTE**
>
> Although the environmental permitting regime covers emissions to all three environmental media, it is worth knowing some of the details and background (covered below) to add to your answers on water pollution.

Section 90A Consents to discharge

The details of consents to discharge were inserted into the WRA 1991 by Schedule 22 to the Environment Act 1995, which gave the Environment Agency the power to decide all of the details about the form and approval of applications. However, Schedule 28 to the Permitting Regulations repealed this with effect from April 2010, and consents to discharge are now encompassed within the environmental permitting regime.

Sections 34–37 Licences to abstract

Controlling abstraction of water is an important tool in managing pollution levels as, if more water is abstracted before pollutants are added, then the concentration of pollutants will be higher (and potentially harmful). Equally, if water is abstracted after the pollutants have been added, there is a potentially increased risk of those pollutants coming into contact with humans.

Licences are required to abstract by:

- occupier of land adjacent to inland water;
- occupier of land above underground strata from which water is drawn; and
- water undertakers from watercourses.

Exceptions are set out in ss. 27, 27A and 29 WRA, and include an occupier of land through which water flows for domestic and agricultural purposes, up to a maximum of 20 m^3 a day.

Water pollution offences

Along with consents to discharge, the Permitting Regulations have replaced the previous provisions relating to water pollution offences. These were found under s. 85 WRA and, although no longer in force, are worth knowing in order to trace the development of this area of law. The main provision was s. 85(1) WRA, which stated that 'a person contravenes this section if he causes or knowingly permits any poisonous, noxious or polluting matter or any solid waste matter to enter any controlled waters'.

The current rules are set out in various places in the Permitting Regulations, but hinge around regulation 38, which makes it an offence to 'contravene Regulation 12(1) or cause or knowingly permit the contravention of Regulation 12(1)(a)'. Regulation 12, in turn, states that 'a person must not, except under and to the extent authorised by an environmental permit (a) operate a regulated facility; or (b) cause or knowingly permit a water discharge activity or groundwater activity'.

To reiterate, the case law on the meanings of the offences established under the WRA remains the same, but it is now only the Permitting Regulations which apply to pollution offences themselves.

KEY DEFINITION: Water discharge activity

A 'water discharge activity' means any of the following –

(a) the discharge or entry to inland freshwaters, coastal waters or relevant territorial waters of any –

(i) poisonous, noxious or polluting matter,

(ii) waste matter, or

(iii) trade effluent or sewage effluent;

(b) the discharge from land through a pipe into the sea outside the seaward limits of relevant territorial waters of any trade effluent or sewage effluent;

(c) the removal from any part of the bottom, channel or bed of any inland freshwaters of a deposit accumulated by reason of any dam, weir or sluice holding back the waters, by causing it to be carried away in suspension in the waters, unless the activity is carried on in the exercise of a power conferred by or under any enactment relating to land drainage, flood prevention or navigation;

(d) the cutting or uprooting of a substantial amount of vegetation in any inland freshwaters or so near to any such waters that it falls into them and failure to take reasonable steps to remove the vegetation from these waters.

(Para. 3, Sch. 21 Environmental Permitting (England and Wales) Regulations 2010/675)

This is similar but wider than the offences listed under s. 85 WRA and, as a new provision, there has yet to be any case law or academic comment relating directly to it.

Some of the words used in the new regime are the same as previous provisions, notably 'cause or knowingly permit' and 'poisonous, noxious or polluting matter'. These are phrases that predate the WRA, and there is a body of case law that has built up around what they mean. Since *Houston* v *Buchanan* [1940] 2 All ER 179, the two parts of the offence have been read disjunctively: that is to say, 'causing' is one offence, and 'knowingly permitting' is another.

KEY CASE

Alphacell v *Woodward* [1972] AC 824

Concerning: intention; pollution; rivers; strict liability; causing

Facts

Polluting matter entered a river from settling tanks as a result of blockage of a pump strainer by 'brambles ferns and leaves'. The tanks had been inspected prior to the overflow and found to be working properly.

Legal principle

'Causes' was to be given a common-sense meaning. The appellants had caused the polluting matter to enter the river since the complex operation, which had led inevitably in the event of the pumps not operating properly to polluting matter entering the river, had been deliberately conducted by them. Furthermore a defect in one stage of it, even assuming that that had happened without negligence on their part, could not enable them to say that they had not 'caused' the polluting matter to enter the river.

✎ EXAM TIP

Consider the changes made by the Permitting Regulations, and the impact these might have on some of the decided cases under s. 85 WRA such as *R* v *Dovermoss Ltd* [1995] Env LR 258, *National Rivers Authority* v *Egger UK Ltd* (1992) Water Law 169, *Re Attorney-General's Reference (No. 1 of 1994)* [1995] 1 WLR 599.

Which water is protected?

Under the WRA, controlled waters were defined in s. 104, and these meanings have been carried over verbatim to the Permitting Regulations under Water Discharge Activities (Para. 3, Sch. 21), although s. 104(1)(d) on groundwater pollution has become Paragraph 3 of Schedule 22 to the Permitting Regulations.

In *R* v *Dovermoss* [1995] Env LR 258, it was argued, unsuccessfully, that water could only be categorised as being in a relevant watercourse when it had become floodwater. Stuart Smith LJ stated that 'water that overflows from a river, stream or ditch does not cease to be water of the watercourse' (p. 263) and added that 'watercourses such as these [rivers, streams, ditches] do not cease to be watercourses simply because they are dry at any particular times' (p. 263).

> **! Don't be tempted to . . .**
>
> Be wary of assuming that the Permitting Regulations have merely consolidated previous legislation. Even though much of the framework has been carried forward from the WRA, there are several important amendments that have been made.

Defences

The defences to a charge under s. 85 WRA were based on ss. 88 and 89 WRA. The essence of s. 88 WRA is that the discharge had been authorised by one of a list of provisions, and thus no offence could have taken place. Section 89 WRA has effectively been transposed (with minor changes) into Regulation 40 of the Permitting Regulations, and hinges around the argument that the 'acts alleged to constitute the contravention were done in an emergency in order to avoid danger to human health.' As such, the case law which has arisen around s. 89 WRA still holds good.

> **KEY CASE**
>
> *Impress (Worcester) Ltd* v *Rees* [1971] 2 All ER 357
>
> *Concerning: statutory duty; third parties; vicarious liability; water pollution*
>
> **Facts**
>
> A fuel storage tank valve was opened by an unknown person at night, causing fuel to enter a river.
>
> **Legal principle**
>
> A party cannot 'cause' pollution of a river, where the pollution is due to the action of an unauthorised person done for purposes unconnected with that party's business.

There is no reason to suggest that the new regulations will make any difference to this defence, which is effectively that of *novus actus interveniens*, or a break in the chain of causation.

KEY CASE

Environment Agency (formerly National Rivers Authority) v *Empress Car Co (Abertillery) Ltd* [1997] Env LR 227

Concerning: causation; water pollution

Facts

Diesel escaped from a tank via an unlocked tap into a storm drain and then into a river. The person or persons responsible for opening the tap was unknown, although Empress Car Co suggested it might have been trespassers.

Legal principle

Per Schiemann, LJ at 228–9:

1. to be guilty of causing, the defendant need not be shown to be the sole cause of an event;
2. to be guilty of causing, the defendant need not know or foresee the consequence of his acts, omissions or role;
3. where there are a number of possible causes the question which the court ought to ask itself is whether the intervening cause, competing cause or other cause (as the case may be) is of such a powerful nature that the conduct of the defendant cannot amount to a cause at all in the circumstances of the case;
4. whether the conduct of the defendant amounts to causing is a matter of common sense for the adjudicating tribunal on the facts of any particular case.

A second defence, which existed under s. 89(1)(a) WRA, was that of the polluting matter entering controlled water as a result of 'an emergency in order to prevent harm to human health'.

KEY CASE

Express Ltd (t/a Express Dairies Distribution) v *Environment Agency* [2003] EWHC 448 (Admin)

Concerning: causation; defences; offences; water pollution

Facts

A tyre blow-out on a milk tanker led to damage to the tanker which, in turn, led to milk entering controlled water. Express argued that the chain of causation had been broken, and that the 'emergency' defence in s. 89(1) WRA applied.

Legal principle

Hale LJ said 'it is quite impossible to say that the chain of causation from start to finish was broken' and the emergency defence did apply.

Make your answer stand out

Even though s. 85 WRA is no longer current, Parpworth (2009) gives a detailed exploration of liability under that section. Since the aspects of s. 85 WRA which are dealt with in his article carry forward into the new regime, this is still a very useful resource.

The Water Framework Directive

Directive 2000/60/EC establishing a framework for the Community action in the field of water policy (the Water Framework Directive, WFD) was intended to create an overall framework for water across the EU, which meant that integrated and coherent water policies would have to be developed by national authorities. McEldowney and McEldowney call the WFD 'one of the most significant and innovative approaches fostered by the European Union' (2010: 266) and, as is to be expected by a framework directive, the WFD set out consolidate a number of existing directives over a period of time. The first two of the consolidating daughter directives, on groundwater and priority substances, are discussed below.

The general objective of the WFD is set out by the European Commission's DG Environment as 'protection of the aquatic ecology, specific protection of unique and valuable habitats, protection of drinking water resources, and protection of bathing water'.

One of the fundamental changes wrought by the WFD was that water should no longer be administered along political or administrative boundaries, but by management plans set out on the basis of river basins. Article 3(3) of the WFD designates a river basin crossing the territory of two or more member states as an international river basin district, and Article 3(5) sets out how member states should negotiate with non-member states if a river basin extends beyond the EU.

The latter provision is of no concern in the UK, where the WFD was implemented by the Water Environment (Water Framework Directive) (England and Wales) Regulations 2003, and there are 16 river basin districts (including three international river basin districts crossing the border between northern Ireland and the Republic of Ireland).

The EA consultation on River Basin Management Plans closed in December 2012, and in 2013, the EA published guidance on 'Water for Life and Livelihoods: Managing water for people, business, agriculture and the environment' which included responses to the consultation, and set out general plans for the future. The EA also says that they 'are now reviewing and updating the [River Basin Management] plans for England, and will publish the revised plans in December 2015'.

The Groundwater Daughter Directive

Directive 2006/118/EC on the protection of groundwater against pollution and deterioration will repeal Directive 80/68/EC on the protection of groundwater against pollution caused by certain dangerous substances on 22 December 2013, and member states had until 15 January 2009 to transpose the Directive into national law.

The Directive was implemented in the UK through the Groundwater (England and Wales) Regulations 2009, although these have subsequently been repealed by Schedule 22 of the Permitting Regulations, which deals with issues relating to groundwater pollution.

The Priority Substances Daughter Directive

In addition to measures designed to protect groundwater, the WFD established a 'priority list' of substances posing a threat to or via the aquatic environment. Directive 2008/105/EC on environmental quality standards in the field of water policy, the transposition deadline for which was 13 July 2010, and the River Basin Districts Typology, Standards and Groundwater Threshold Values (Water Framework Directive) (England and Wales) Directions 2010 were published by the Secretary of State under powers given by s. 122(2) Environment Act 1995 to instruct the EA on implementation measures.

 Make your answer stand out

For a recent and interesting comparison of the way in which the WFD is being implemented across a range of EU member states, Keessen et al. suggest that there is a two-speed system developing in the EU, and that the ambitions of the more ambitious member states may be harmed by 'unambitious national practices' (2010: 221) of other member states. In an article which covers the WFD and other non-water Directives, Jack (2011) states that the Commission is failing in its role as enforcer because of lack of resources.

■ Putting it all together

Answer guidelines

See the essay question at the start of the chapter. A diagram illustrating how to structure your answer is available on the companion website.

Approaching the question

The question is asking you to assess two things – water quality controls in the UK before the WFD and those that were brought into play because of the WFD. You will then need to contrast the two sets of controls and come to a conclusion.

Important points to include

- Although you could go back to very early controls, your answer will be constrained by time and/or size limits, so it would make more sense to take the WRA 1991 as a starting point.

- Decide which aspects of water quality control are to be the basis of your answer – classification, standards, enforcement, for example, or elements of all three. This will have great impact on the focus of the rest of your answer.

- Clearly you will need to bring in appropriate case law, and the sections of statute that applied at the time, but also make reference to National Rivers Authority and Environment Agency publications, RCEP reports, and the relevant journal articles that discuss them.

- The section on the WFD could give some background to it, but be careful not to spend too long on this as, although it is useful, it is not the focus of the question. You should look instead at what the WFD was introduced to do, and how that has been achieved in the UK.

- You should also look at any criticisms of the WFD – either in terms of content, speed or implementation.

 Make your answer stand out

Depending on your focus for the answer, look at the arguments put forward by Keessen et al. (2010), Jack (2011) and Howarth (2011) about potential problems with the WFD approach.

READ TO IMPRESS

EA (2013) *Water for Life and Livelihoods: Managing water for people, business, agriculture and the environment*, Bristol: Environment Agency

Howarth, W. (2011) Diffuse water pollution and diffuse environmental laws, *J. Env. L.* 23(1), 129–41

Jack, B. (2011) Enforcing member state compliance with EU environmental law: a critical evaluation of the use of financial penalties, *J. Env. L.* 23(1), 73–95

Keessen, A., van Kempen, J., van Rijswick, M., Robbe, J. and Backes, C. (2010) European river basin districts: are they swimming in the same implementation pool? *J. Env. L.* 22(2), 197–221

McEldowney, P. and McEldowney, S. (2010) *Environmental Law*, Harlow: Longman

Parpworth, N. (2009) Who may be liable for an offence contrary to s. 85 of the Water Resources Act 1991? *J.P.L.* 3, 294–309

RCEP (1972) *Pollution in some British Estuaries and Coastal Waters*, Royal Commission on Environmental Pollution, 3rd Report, London: HMSO

Vörösmarty, C., McIntyre, P., Gessner, M., Dudgeon, D., Prusevich, A., Green, P., Glidden, S., Bunn, S., Sullivan, C., Reidy Liermann, C. and Davies, P. (2010) Global threats to human water security and river biodiversity, *Nature* 467, 555–61

Wolf, S. and Stanley, N. (2010) *Wolf and Stanley on Environmental Law*, 5th Edn. London: Routledge

www.pearsoned.co.uk/lawexpress

 Go online to access more revision support including quizzes to test your knowledge, sample questions with answer guidelines, podcasts you can download, and more!

Waste management

9

Revision checklist

Essential points you should know:

- [ ] What waste is
- [ ] How waste is managed at different levels (e.g. extra-national, EU, UK)
- [ ] The waste hierarchy

■ Topic map

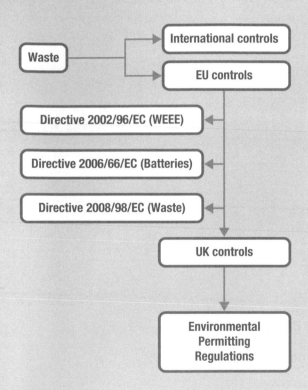

■ Introduction

All countries, cities and individuals produce waste, and they always will.

'The idea of waste is not necessarily associated with pollution – although all pollution is associated with waste' (Bell, McGillivray and Pedersen, 2013: 682). This area of law is concerned with making sure that the levels of waste produced are controlled as well as possible, and that any waste which is produced is dealt with in a way which minimises the adverse effects on the environment. The UK's obligations in this area originate under a number of international treaties, predominantly under the auspices of the UN, and these have also influenced and guided EU law. Waste management is a vast topic, and so it is outside the scope of this text to cover all aspects of the law relating to waste management. Where applicable, suggestions for wider reading will allow you to investigate some of the areas for yourself.

Although hazardous waste is now dealt with at an EU level by Directive 2008/98/EC on waste, along with non-hazardous waste, the specific regulations relating to the disposal and transportation of hazardous waste are dealt with at the end of the chapter.

ASSESSMENT ADVICE

This is an area which could be assessed equally well by problem questions or essay questions. Whichever type of question you are given, make sure you understand the type of waste that is being discussed, and both the potential further uses it might have and the level of risk it poses to the environment.

■ Sample question

Could you answer this question? Below is a typical essay question that could arise on this topic. Guidelines on answering the question are included at the end of this chapter, whilst a sample problem question and guidance on tackling it can be found on the companion website.

ESSAY QUESTION

Consider critically the difficulties that have arisen in defining the concept of 'waste' and the particular difficulty that one person's waste may be another's valuable source material.

Waste

One of the issues that emerges repeatedly in debates and case law concerning waste is what actually counts as waste. The key definitions, set out below, appear relatively straightforward, but they allow considerable room for manoeuvre. Recently, the Environmental Protection Act (EPA) 1990 definition of waste has been amended by the Waste (England and Wales) Regulations 2011 and now refers directly to the definition in Directive 2008/98/EC.

KEY DEFINITION: Waste

Directive 2008/98/EC on Waste, Article 3(a):

'waste' means any substance or object which the holder discards or intends or is required to discard.

The EU definition of waste, which has its roots in that given in Directive 75/442/EEC on waste, is partly assessed from the perspective of the 'holder' of the substance or object, and this means that it is relatively common for things which are capable of economical reuse being treated as waste. In the case of *Environment Agency* v *Inglenorth Ltd* [2009] EWHC 670 (Admin) the arguments centred on whether or not 'a thing' could be counted as 'discarded' (and therefore waste), and thus whether a prosecution for being an unlicensed waste transporter could stand. Similarly, the ECJ case of *Palin Granit Oy* (below) shows that the Directive definition of 'waste' can be applied rather broadly.

KEY CASE

Case C-9/00 Palin Granit Oy v *Vehmassalon kansanterveystyön kuntayhtymän hallitus* **[2002] Env LR 35**

Concerning: waste management; definition of 'waste'; whether residual stone left at quarry was 'production residue' where reuse of stone was uncertain

Facts

Palin Granit Oy (PG) was granted a licence in Finland to store leftover stone from quarrying with a view to using it for gravel at an unspecified future date. The Finnish Administrative Court held it was 'waste' and that storage required a landfill licence.

Legal principle

The leftover stone might have had a subsidiary use, but it was 'not certain and only foreseeable in the longer term' and was thus essentially an extraction residue. It was therefore to be classified as waste within the meaning of the Directive.

Once a substance has been declared to be waste, it can then be classified into one of a myriad of different types of waste, according to the consolidated European Waste Catalogue (EWC). The EWC uses a six-digit code for classifying waste, and this allows for very specific treatment to be aligned to specific types of waste. There are 20 categories of waste under the EWC, and category 03 for example is 'Wastes from wood processing and the production of panels and furniture, pulp, paper and cardboard.' Within category 03, there are three sub-categories, and within these there are 19 further divisions. Thus category 03 01 01 is 'waste bark and cork', 03 01 02 is 'sawdust, shavings, cuttings, wood, particle board and veneer containing dangerous substances', and so on. The EWC is further refined by some of the entries being additionally classified as 'Absolute Entries' ('hazardous waste regardless of any threshold concentrations') or 'Mirror Entries' ('hazardous waste only if dangerous substances are present above threshold concentrations').

> **! Don't be tempted to . . .**
>
> A common mistake in questions concerning the definition of waste is to assume that just because something is listed in the EWC it is automatically 'waste'. Don't forget the subjective aspect as well – that the holder must also treat it as though it is waste.

This leads to what Bell, McGillivray and Pedersen call a 'high level of environmental protection by making the definition of waste contextual – that is, by basing it on the intention of the holder – while the detailed categories provide a degree of detail that clarifies the general definition' (2013: 683).

> **📖 REVISION NOTE**
>
> Throughout this chapter, be aware of the impacts that the Environmental Permitting (England and Wales) Regulations 2010 (as discussed in Chapter 6), will have on waste production by large-scale polluters.

■ Extra-national controls

The 1972 Oslo Convention for the Prevention of Marine Pollution by Dumping from Ships and Aircraft prohibited the dumping of Annex I ('black list') substances (those with a high potential for damaging the environment on account of their toxicity, persistence or bio-accumulation) in the North Sea and North East Atlantic. The Convention also obliged a permit system to be introduced for other, specified wastes. It was initially fulfilled in the UK by the Dumping at Sea Act 1974 and the Food and Environment Protection Act 1985. The Oslo Convention was extended in 1974 by the Paris Convention for the Prevention of Marine Pollution from Land-Based Sources which covered land-based sources and the offshore industry. The Water Industry Act 1991 gave effect to the Paris Convention in the UK.

Both of these conventions, the scope of which was limited to the North Sea and North Atlantic, were replaced in 1992 by the Convention for the Protection of the Marine Environment of the North-East Atlantic (OSPAR Convention), Articles 3, 4 and 5 of which compel signatory states to take 'individually and jointly, all possible steps to prevent and eliminate pollution' from land-based sources, dumping or incineration, or offshore sources respectively.

In 1973, the London Convention on Prevention of Marine Pollution by Dumping of Wastes and Other Matter was passed, which also bans the marine dumping of substances included on a 'black list'. Where the Oslo, Paris and OSPAR Conventions are all limited geographically, the London Convention extends to 'all marine waters other than the internal waters of States' (Art. III(3)).

The United Kingdom is a signatory both to OSPAR and to the London Convention.

 Make your answer stand out

All of the conventions mentioned above forbid the dumping of waste into the sea (either completely, or without certain permits). Elsewhere, carbon capture and storage (CCS) is much in favour as a way of reducing the effects of climate change. If you were to consider this in light of plans to store CO_2 in the sea-bed, it would impress the examiners. See, for example, Dixon et al., who discuss ways round the potential conflicts, saying there is 'uncertainty with different legal interpretations on different aspects of the issue' (2009: 4504).

■ Extra-national controls: European Union

Chapter 3 (on sources and concepts of environmental law) has shown how the EU Treaty has been amended to include environmental protection under Article 191, and also the impact of the various Environmental Action Programmes.

One of the seven 'thematic strategies' of the 6th EAP is 'Waste Prevention and Recycling' and Article 8 of the Decision laying down the programme sets out four objectives of the waste strategy:

1. breaking the linkage between economic growth and energy use;
2. waste prevention;
3. reduction in waste going to disposal HW production; and
4. increased re-use and recycling, and ensuring safe disposal of waste.

The old Waste Framework Directive (Directive 75/442/EEC) was replaced by the new Waste Directive (Directive 2008/98/EC) but much of the structure remains unchanged. Article 4 sets out the 'Waste Hierarchy' which lays down the approach governments should take in drawing up waste strategies. The UK government published a review of waste policy in June 2011 (Defra, 2011), the Action Plan for which calls for the development of a new National Waste Prevention Programme to be produced by 2013. The consultation for this was launched by Defra on 6 August 2013, and closed at the end of September 2013.

KEY STATUTE

Article 4, Directive 2008/98/EC on Waste

(1) The following waste hierarchy shall apply as a priority order in waste prevention and management legislation and policy:

    (a) prevention;

    (b) preparing for re-use;

    (c) recycling;

    (d) other recovery, e.g. energy recovery; and

    (e) disposal.

(2) When applying the waste hierarchy referred to in paragraph 1, Member States shall take measures to encourage the options that deliver the best overall environmental outcome. This may require specific waste streams departing from the hierarchy where this is justified by life-cycle thinking on the overall impacts of the generation and management of such waste.

The current Waste Strategy for England (2007) sets a range of 'targets and indicators' for different sources of waste by 2020:

Household waste recycling:	50%
Household residual waste:	45% reduction from 2000 levels
Municipal waste recovery:	75%

The Strategy also sets out a target to reduce by 2010 the amount of commercial and industrial waste that is sent to landfill by 20 per cent of the 2004 levels. Defra is currently running a consultation process on a new waste prevention programme for England, following its 2011 review of Waste Policy. The new programme is due to be published in December 2013.

Waste electrical and electronic equipment

Directive 2002/96/EC on waste electrical and electronic equipment (the WEEE Directive) and its 'sister' Directive (2011/65/EU on the restriction on the use of certain hazardous substances in electrical and electronic equipment) require systems to be put into place for the recovery and suitable treatment of waste electrical and electronic equipment (WEEE).

The WEEE Directive is a framework, setting general principles for collection, recycling and financing of redundant, end-of-life and scrap equipment, but giving national leeway as to implementation detail. Its objectives are to reduce the quantities of waste being disposed, and the harmfulness of what is disposed and to preserve natural resources and save energy.

In accordance with the 'polluter pays' principle, the legislation requires original producers to pay the costs of recycling products from domestic households and obliges them to establish, or participate in, formal collection schemes.

The WEEE Directive was transposed in UK by the Waste Electrical and Electronic Equipment Regulations 2006. Schedules 1 and 2 to the Regulations repeat Annexes 1 and 1B of the Directive, and set out categories of electrical and electronic equipment and individual product types covered by the Regulations.

Such products will now have to be marked with the crossed-out wheelie bin symbol, the name of the producer and the date of being put on to the market. All producers who put EEE on the market in the UK are responsible for financing the costs of the collection, treatment, recovery and environmentally sound disposal of WEEE and must join an approved compliance scheme. Operators of such schemes have certain reporting, compliance and record-keeping responsibilities.

Regulation 31 states that EEE distributors must provide an in-store take-back service or subscribe to an approved distributor take-back scheme. Distributors must also provide the following information to purchasers (reg. 33):

(a) the requirement on each member state under Article 2 of the Directive to minimise the disposal of WEEE as unsorted municipal waste and to achieve a high level of collection of WEEE for treatment, recovery and environmentally sound disposal;

(b) the collection and take-back systems available to them;

(c) their role in contributing to the reuse, recycling and other forms of recovery of WEEE under these Regulations;

(d) the potential effects on the environment and human health as a result of the presence of hazardous substances in EEE; and

(e) the meaning of the crossed-out wheelie bin symbol.

Batteries

Directive 2006/66/EC on batteries and accumulators and waste batteries and accumulators prohibits the placing on the market of certain batteries and accumulators containing mercury or cadmium (most batteries containing > 0.0005 per cent mercury or > 0.002 per cent cadmium), and promotes a high level of collection and recycling of waste batteries and accumulators and improved environmental performance of all operators involved in the life cycle. The waste element of the Directive was given effect in the UK by the Waste Batteries and Accumulators Regulations 2009.

There are various targets that have been set in order to achieve these goals. Collection targets for portable batteries (by sales) were 25 per cent by 2012 and are 45 per cent by 2016.

This is bolstered by the requirement on retailers that they must take back portable batteries (Reg. 31), on producers of industrial batteries to take back waste industrial batteries (Reg. 35) and on producers to take back private vehicle batteries (Reg. 36). All of this must be done free of charge, regardless of whether a new battery is bought.

There are separate targets for producers of batteries to recycle and treat them.

Recycling targets (by weight, by September 2011) are 65 per cent (lead-acid batteries), 75 per cent (NiCd batteries), and 50 per cent (other batteries).

Disposal of industrial and automotive batteries and accumulators to landfill or by incineration is also prohibited (Reg. 56), although portable batteries containing cadmium, mercury or lead can be disposed of in landfills or underground storage if there is no viable end market available or if these methods are part of a strategy to phase out heavy metals, and disposal is shown to be preferable to recycling on the grounds of environmental, economic and/or social impact.

■ Duty of care

The idea of a duty of care being applied to those involved in the broader process of waste was introduced in s. 34 of the Environmental Protection Act 1990. It is still often referred to as the 's. 34 Duty of Care'. The offences which are to be prevented are listed in s. 33 'Prohibition on unauthorised or harmful deposit, treatment or disposal etc. of waste'.

KEY STATUTE

Environmental Protection Act 1990 (as amended and applying in England and Wales)

Section 34 Duty of Care etc. as respects waste:

(1) Subject to ss. (2) below, it shall be the duty of any person who imports, produces, carries, keeps, treats or disposes of controlled waste or, as a dealer or broker, has control of such waste, to take all such measures applicable to him in that capacity as are reasonable in the circumstances –

  (a) to prevent any contravention by any other person of s. 33 above;

    (aa) to prevent any contravention by any other person of regulation 12 of the Environmental Permitting Regulations or of a condition of an environmental permit;

  (b) to prevent the escape of the waste from his control or that of any other person; and ▶

> (c) on the transfer of the waste, to secure –
>
> > (i) that the transfer is only to an authorised person or to a person for authorised transport purposes; and
> >
> > (ii) that there is transferred such a written description of the waste as will enable other persons to avoid a contravention of that section or regulation 12 of the Environmental Permitting Regulations, or a contravention of a condition of an environmental permit, and to comply with the duty under this subsection as respects the escape of waste.

The duty applies to all who have defined responsibility at any stage of the process, and it is specific as to each person's role in the events. The main qualification of the duty is that it is not absolute; it is only to 'act reasonably'.

The duty was extended to householders by the Waste (Household Duty of Care) (England and Wales) Regulations 2005, which inserted s. 2A:

> (2A) It shall be the duty of the occupier of any domestic property in England to take all such measures available to him as are reasonable in the circumstances to secure that any transfer by him of household waste produced on the property is only to an authorised person or to a person for authorised transport purposes.

In practice, this means that individuals have a duty to ensure that others who are involved in the waste chain – let alone themselves – do not break the law. You must also be vigilant over the actions of others, as it is not enough to think that you are handing over your duty of care to someone else when you hand over your waste to them.

Duty of care: authorised persons and transport of waste

Authorised persons (to give waste to) are listed in s. 34(3), and the only exception to the duty to pass waste to authorised persons is if it is for 'authorised transport purposes' which are listed in s. 34(4).

Waste carriers must be registered, under a regime which dates back to the Control of Pollution (Amendment) Act 1989, s. 1 of which provides that: 'it shall be an offence for any person who is not a registered carrier of controlled waste, in the course of any business of his or otherwise with a view to profit, to transport any controlled waste to or from any place in Great Britain.'

▌ Landfill

Directive 1999/31/EC on the Landfill of Waste (the Landfill Directive) is the source of current EU law and landfill. It was transposed into UK law almost a year late, by the Landfill (England

and Wales) Regulations 2002. These were amended several times, and the area is now subject to the provisions of the Environmental Permitting (England and Wales) Regulations 2010 (the Permitting Regulations; see Chapter 6 on environmental permitting).

The Directive separates all waste into three categories – hazardous, non-hazardous and inert (Art. 4), and introduced provisions to reduce the landfilling of biodegradable municipal wastes (Art. 5). The targets are to reduce the quantity (by weight) to 75 per cent (of 1995 levels) by 2006, 50 per cent by 2009 and 35 per cent by 2016.

For all of these targets, the UK opted for a derogation in the target dates for an additional four years.

In the UK, a pair of regulations set out this regime. The Landfill (Scheme Year and Maximum Landfill Amount) Regulations 2004 set maximum limits for the amount of biodegradable waste for landfill, and the Landfill Allowances and Trading Scheme (England) Regulations 2004 (LATS) imposed landfill targets for local authorities. LATS also set out mechanisms to implement the regime, the provisions regarding the borrowing, banking and trading of allowances and set a penalty (of £150 per tonne) if the allowances are exceeded by a particular local authority.

In November 2006, Defra announced that every local authority had managed to meet its LATS targets with only ten of them throughout England and Wales having to buy from other authorities. It also announced that the total amount of household waste had fallen for the first time as had the total amount of such waste being landfilled.

Article 6 of the Directive states that the only waste type that can be landfilled is inert waste and waste that has been subject to treatment. Treatment is defined as:

> the physical, chemical or biological processes, including sorting, that change the characteristics of the waste in order to reduce its volume or hazardous nature, facilitate its handling or enhance recovery (Art. 2(h)).

Landfill sites classified as 'hazardous' (under Art. 4) will only be allowed to accept hazardous wastes; those classified as 'non-hazardous' will only be allowed to accept municipal and other non-hazardous wastes and stabilised, non-reactive (e.g. vitrified, solidified, etc.) hazardous wastes; and those classified as 'inert' will only be allowed to accept inert wastes.

▪ Hazardous waste

Internationally, the regulation of Hazardous Waste (HW) is dominated by one thing – the 1989 Basel Convention on the Control of Transboundary Movements of Hazardous Wastes and their Disposal. The Convention came about as a result of several incidences of developed countries exporting their HW to the developing world, where the facilities for safely dealing with it did not exist. As a result, the Convention established a control system generally involving 'prior informed consent' of the prospective importing state for a range of 'hazardous' wastes. It has been ratified by 176 countries. There is an amendment (the 'Ban Amendment') to the Basel Convention, which was adopted in 1995 and would prohibit the export of all hazardous waste from developed countries to developing countries. It has been signed by 70 countries but, due to disagreement on the entry into force criteria, it is not yet legally in force.

In the EU, the Basel Convention is currently given effect by Regulation 1013/2006 on shipments of waste which, although it is only directly concerned with transboundary movements, does state that:

> national systems concerning shipments of waste should take account of the need for coherence with the Community system in order to ensure a high level of protection of the environment and human health (Preamble 13).

Regulation 1013/2006 also carries forward the EU's adoption of the Ban Amendment, which therefore does have effect within the EU.

Although the preceding measures have dealt with the transport of HW, they do not deal with the disposal of such waste. Directive 2008/98/EC on waste ('the Waste Directive') defines 'hazardous waste' by reference to 'one or more of the hazardous properties listed in Annex III' which is partially reproduced below.

Properties of waste which render it hazardous (Annex III of the Waste Directive)

Class	Property
H1	Explosive
H2	Oxidizing
H3-A	Highly flammable (flash point below 21°C)
H3-B	Flammable (flash point between 21°C and 55°C)
H4	Irritant
H5	Harmful
H6	Toxic
H7	Carcinogenic
H8	Corrosive
H9	Infectious
H10	Toxic for reproduction
H11	Mutagenic
H12	Waste which releases toxic/very toxic gases in contact with water, air or acid

Class	Property
H13	Sensitising substances and preparations which, if they are inhaled or if they penetrate the skin, are capable of eliciting a reaction of hypersensitization such that on further exposure to the substance or preparation, characteristic adverse effects are produced
H14	Ecotoxic
H15	Waste capable by any means, after disposal, of yielding another substance, e.g. a leachate, which possesses any of the characteristics listed above

The remainder of the HW provisions of the Waste Directive are covered in Articles 17–20. Article 17 is a general duty on member states to ensure that HW is dealt with safely and records are kept accurately.

Article 18 is a ban on the mixing of HW and other types of HW or other types of waste, unless it is carried out under a permit. Mixing include dilution.

Article 19 concerns the proper labelling of HW and the documentation that needs to be completed on transfer of HW within a member state.

Article 20 gives an exemption for 'mixed waste produced by households'.

In the UK, the current provisions are in the Hazardous Waste (England and Wales) Regulations 2005, although certain sections have been amended by the Waste (England and Wales) Regulations 2011. Although the title would lead you to think that the regulation extended to England and Wales, in fact the only provision that extends to Wales are certain amendments to the Environmental Protection Act 1990. In fact, there are now separate but broadly complementary regimes in Wales (Hazardous Waste) (Wales) Regulations 2005, Scotland (Waste) (Scotland) Regulations 2011 and Northern Ireland (Waste) (Northern Ireland) Regulations 2011. The reminder of this section will focus on the English Regulations.

Parts 1 to 3 define hazardous waste and set out how the regulations apply. The definition of hazardous waste in Regulation 6 refers to the list of hazardous wastes set out in the List of Wastes (England) Regulations 2005.

Part 4 bans the mixing of HW, and Part 5 makes it an offence to remove HW from premises which have not been notified to the Environment Agency, unless they are exempt premises or the waste has been flytipped.

Parts 6 and 7 deal with the documentation required to move HW and record-keeping by those who move it.

Because of the differing regimes in the UK, Schedule 7 covers the requirements for the importation into England of HW from Scotland and Northern Ireland and *vice versa*, and effectively recognises the consignment notes of the respective regulations applicable in those countries.

In any answer on waste, keep in mind that, according to the figures released by Defra in 2011, total waste generation in the UK in 2008 was 288.6mt. Household waste accounted for 10.9 per cent (31.5mt), compared to 35 per cent for construction (101mt), 30 per cent for mining and quarrying (86mt) and 23 per cent for other commercial and industrial waste (67.3mt). Also, hazardous waste accounted for just over 2 per cent of waste.

■ Putting it all together

Answer guidelines

See the essay question at the start of the chapter.

Approaching the question

This question clearly relates to the issue of definitions, and you should decide before you start whether you are going to focus on the subjective aspects of the definition or the categorisation of wastes, or both.

Important points to include

- Ideally, you should begin by looking at the statutory definitions of waste that are used in the UK and EU. This will give you a firm basis on which to base the remainder of your answer.

- Make the point that there are two aspects to the definition and classification, and that it is the treatment of a substance by the holder as waste that is crucial. There is case law you can bring in at this point, particularly the case of *Environment Agency* v *Inglenorth Ltd* [2009] EWHC 670 (Admin) which links to the question well.

- You can also decide whether you are going to focus the rest of your answer on one specific type of waste (e.g. hazardous or inert), or to keep looking at waste in general.

- An advantage of focusing on one type is that you will be able to be much more precise in finding and analysing any problems that have arisen, but the disadvantage may be that you will have to extrapolate very specific answers into a wider conclusion, which is rarely recommended.

Make your answer stand out

To impress the examiners, you could include a very topical discussion on the issue of energy from waste, and the planning and other problems that surround this. Ogley (2011), for example, argues that the 'proximity principle' under the Waste Directive is being over-zealously applied, at the cost to the environment.

READ TO IMPRESS

Bell, S., McGillivray, D. and Pedersen, O. (2013) *Environmental Law*, 8th Edn. Oxford: Oxford University Press

Defra (2011) *Government Review of Waste Policy in England 2011*, Department for Environment Food and Rural Affairs, Report PB 13540, London: TSO

Dixon, T., Greaves, A., Christopherson, O., Vivian, C. and Thomson, J. (2009) International marine regulation of CO_2 geological storage, developments and implications of London and OSPAR, *Energy Procedia* 1, 4503–10

Ogley, A. (2011) A wasted opportunity, *JPL* 1, 10–13

www.pearsoned.co.uk/lawexpress

 Go online to access more revision support including quizzes to test your knowledge, sample questions with answer guidelines, podcasts you can download, and more!

Nature conservation and landscape management

Revision checklist

Essential points you should know:

- [ ] What conservation is
- [ ] Protection of flora and fauna (e.g. by CITES, EU law)
- [ ] Habitat and ecosystem protection
- [ ] The development of nature conservation law in England and Wales
- [ ] The use of SSSIs and other designations to protect habitat

Topic map

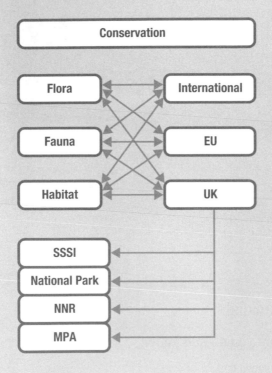

■ Introduction

This is a very important area of environmental law that is often overlooked, but which features in many exam questions.

The conservation of nature and the management of landscape are both potentially vast topic areas, so your particular syllabus may not have covered everything featured in this chapter. The former, with clear links to the concepts of biodiversity and sustainability (which are discussed in Chapter 3 on sources and concepts of environmental law), is driven partly by the fact that it has been estimated that in the last few centuries 128 known species of birds (Norris and Pain, 2002: 105) have become extinct, as have 28 known species of mammals since 1900. As Leakey and Lewin neatly put it, '99.99% of all species that have ever existed on Earth are now extinct' (1996: 39). Both conservation and landscape management also have links to planning law (see Chapter 5), and development generally (sustainable or otherwise) is, in the UK particularly, concerned with managing the often competing demands of business, population, transport and conservation.

ASSESSMENT ADVICE

This topic area lends itself more to essay-type questions than to problem questions, although the latter are possible. Essay questions are likely to focus on aspects such as the different levels of protection afforded to different species, or different types of habitat, and the benefits or otherwise of this.

■ Sample question

Could you answer this question? Below is a typical essay question that could arise on this topic. Guidelines on answering the question are included at the end of this chapter, whilst a sample problem question and guidance on tackling it can be found on the companion website.

ESSAY QUESTION

In light of the modern challenges critically evaluate the various legal mechanisms that have been used in the UK to regulate and protect biodiversity

■ International law

Originally, 'conservation' was perceived both nationally and internationally as a way of obtaining the optimum sustainable resource yield to secure maximum supply of food and other products. The idea of conserving species for their own value, not simply as resources, is comparatively recent.

In 1948, the International Union for Conservancy of Nature (IUCN) was set up, and produced a 'Red List' of endangered species, which was the basis of CITES in 1973 (see below).

International moves relating to conservation are generally regarded as being starting with the 1972 UNCHE (and its Stockholm Declaration). UNCHE set out the principles concerning wildlife conservation in relation to international law. For example:

- Principle 2: Safeguards natural resources (fauna, air, water and land) for the benefit of present and future generations;

- Principle 4: Identifies man's special responsibility to safeguard the heritage of wildlife and habitat.

The Global Environment Assessment Programme (Earthwatch), UN Environment Programme (UNEP) and Environment Fund were also set up under UNCHE. The principles put forward by the UNCHE (and UNEP) were developed by three conservation strategies: the WCS, the WCN and the WCED.

The 1980 World Conservation Strategy (WCS) emphasised that conservation and development are two sides of the same coin (in which the seeds of sustainable development can clearly be seen), and defined 'conservation' as 'managing the use of the environment and natural resources to ensure the maximum sustainable benefits for present and succeeding generations'.

The 1982 World Charter for Nature (WCN) proclaimed principles of conservation by which all human conduct affecting nature should be guided and judged. Article 1 says that 'Nature shall be respected and its essential processes shall not be impaired', and Article 2 calls for the conservation of habitat, as 'the genetic viability on the earth shall not be compromised; the population levels of all life forms, wild and domesticated, must be at least sufficient for their survival'.

The third of the conservation strategies that emerged from the UNCHE was the World Commission on Environmental Development (WCED) which was, in turn, one of the triggers behind the UNCED in 1992.

Although UNCED is rightly famed for the UN Framework Convention on Climate Change and Agenda 21, in terms of wildlife and nature conservation the most relevant result was the UN Convention on Biological Diversity (Biodiversity Convention) which will be addressed below.

The general influence of international law on the environment, and the differences between hard and soft international law were discussed in Chapter 3, on the sources and concepts of environmental law. This section will deal exclusively with hard law treaties, which have been used to resolve specific problems in the area of species protection.

International Convention for the Regulation of Whaling 1946

The preamble to the ICRW starts: 'Recognizing the interest of the nations of the world in safeguarding for future generations the great natural resources represented by the whale stocks.' The Convention created the International Whaling Commission (Art. 3), the purpose of which was to provide for the proper conservation of whale stocks and thus make possible the orderly development of the whaling industry. The convention was signed by 15 countries only, so although the scope of the convention was global, its impact was more limited. Times have changed since the passage of the Convention, and today membership has grown to 89 states.

> **! Don't be tempted to . . .**
>
> Don't assume that just because the number of countries covered by the Whaling Convention has risen sixfold it has been an unqualified success. There are many states which have signed the Convention but have subsequently withdrawn, others which have signed with a reservation, and yet others (notably Japan) who are fully signed-up members of the Commission and continue whaling under the Article VIII 'scientific research' exemption.

French calls the ICRW one of the clearest examples of the approach to international conventions, 'the ability of the State to preserve sovereign discretion in the matter, even if it requires a conscious act to do so' (2009: 280), and argues that this model is repeated in the opt-out procedure on the CITES Convention.

Convention on the International Trade in Endangered Species of Flora and Fauna 1973

CITES is perhaps one of the best-known of all global conventions relating to flora and fauna. As with the ICRW, CITES started off with a low membership of just 10 countries triggering its entry into force on 1 July 1975 (in accordance with Article XXII). By the end of 1976, however, membership had grown to 30 countries and, with the addition of Iraq in February 2014, CITES currently has a membership of 180 countries.

KEY STATUTE

The Convention on the International Trade in Endangered Species of Flora and Fauna 1973

Preamble:

Recognizing that wild fauna and flora in their many beautiful and varied forms are an irreplaceable part of the natural systems of the earth which must be protected for this and the generations to come;

Conscious of the ever-growing value of wild fauna and flora from aesthetic, scientific, cultural, recreational and economic points of view;

Recognizing that peoples and States are and should be the best protectors of their own wild fauna and flora;

Recognizing, in addition, that international co-operation is essential for the protection of certain species of wild fauna and flora against over-exploitation through international trade;

Convinced of the urgency of taking appropriate measures to this end . . .

The purpose of CITES was to ensure that trade in species did not endanger their chances of survival and it did this by placing 'at risk' species into three appendices, and creating a regulatory mechanism for trade in them.

CITES Appendices

Appendix and definition	Numbers of species
Appendix I: Species 'threatened with extinction which are or may be affected by trade' (Art. II(1))	892 Species 39 Sub-species/22 Populations
Appendix II: Species not at immediate risk of extinction but endangered, and will become at risk of extinction if trade is not controlled (Art. II(2))	30,033 Species (of which 28,674 are flora)/26 Sub-species/19 Populations
Appendix III: Species which may need regional, rather than global protection	161 Species 9 Sub-species/1 Population

The comprehensive regulatory system put into place by CITES means that trade between member states, and between member states and the (few remaining) non-member states is all covered, be it import, export or re-export of any specimens. However, as French alludes to above, there is a well-established system contained within CITES under Article XXIII which allows states to ratify the convention whilst making a reservation with regard to 'any species included in Appendix I, II or III' or 'any parts or derivatives specified in relation to a species included in Appendix III'.

Make your answer stand out

Although the CITES approach of listing species and then controlling international trade in them has been the dominant one over the past four decades, it has not been universally applauded, as it does not cover *domestic* trade in endangered species. Lemieux and Clarke (2009) argue that this lacuna has meant that the effect of CITES on reversing the decline in elephant numbers has been muted. Similarly Pires and Clarke argue that 'a substantial domestic trade in wild parrots still exists [in Bolivia], despite the legal prohibitions' (2011: 315). This problem is exacerbated by the fact that most of the species that are listed in Appendices I and II are from the poorer regions of the world. A good discussion of this debate would be sure to impress the examiner.

UN Convention on Biological Diversity

The Biodiversity Convention, which entered into force in December 1993 in accordance with the procedure set out in Article 36, currently has 193 parties, making it 'one of the most widely ratified environmental conventions' (Birnie, Boyle and Redgwell, 2009: 612).

The aims of the Convention and its 'current emphasis on aspirational targets' (Harrop, 2011: 118) are generally expressed in terms of goals, rather than tightly defined objectives, and even the goals are tempered by phrases such as 'in accordance with its particular conditions and capabilities' (Art. 6), 'as far as possible and as appropriate' (Arts. 5, 7, 8, 9, 10, etc.) or 'taking into account the special needs of developing countries' (Art. 12).

Even with the myriad of caveats, in 2010, the *Global Biodiversity Outlook 3* publication admitted that:

> The target agreed by the world's Governments in 2002, 'to achieve by 2010 a significant reduction of the current rate of biodiversity loss at the global, regional and national level as a contribution to poverty alleviation and to the benefit of all life on Earth', has not been met. (GBO3, Executive Summary)

Trouwborst argues that the 'Biodiversity Convention and a number of instruments adopted in UNCED's wake are testimony of a paradigm shift from ad hoc endangered species conservation towards the proactive and holistic conservation and sustainable use of biological diversity' (2009: 424). This shift in approach is echoed at both an EU and national level and discussed further below.

The Biodiversity Convention has been bolstered by two protocols:

- The 2000 Cartagena Protocol (on Biosafety), the purpose of which is to 'contribute to ensuring an adequate level of protection in the field of the safe transfer, handling and use of living modified organisms resulting from modern biotechnology that may have adverse effects on the conservation and sustainable use of biological diversity' (Art. 1).

- The Nagoya Protocol (on Access to Genetic Resources and the Fair and Equitable Sharing of Benefits Arising from their Utilization) which has 92 signatories (January 2014) and will enter into force after the fiftieth ratification (Art. 33).

EU law

The EU is involved in conservation both as signatory to international treaties and as an international law-making organisation. The laws made under the EU Action Programmes may be divided into three main groups, and examples of each will be given:

- protection of specimens and species of flora and fauna;
- protection of habitat and ecosystems;
- comprehensive and integrated protection.

Flora and fauna

The guiding legislation in relation to birds is Directive 2009/147/EC on the conservation of wild birds, which is a codification of all the amendments that had been made to earlier Directives.

The Directive applies to 'all species of naturally occurring birds in the wild state in the European territory of Member States' (Art. 1(1)), and to their 'eggs, nests and habitats' (Art. 1(2)). On a practical note, this means that the Directive is limited geographically and will not cover non-European territory (e.g. the Falkland Islands, the Canary Islands and so on).

Article 2 requires member states to 'take the requisite measures to maintain the population of the species . . . at a level which corresponds in particular to ecological, scientific and cultural requirements' although it does allow for 'economic and recreational requirements' to be taken into account, which allows for considerable leeway.

Much as with CITES, the species that are covered by the Directive are listed in three annexes, and subject to decreasing levels of control.

Annexes to the Birds Directive

Annexe	Coverage	Requirement
1	193 Species (including regular migratory species)	Special conservation measures concerning their habitat in order to ensure their survival and reproduction in their area of distribution (Art. 4(1))
		Prohibition of 'sale, transport for sale, keeping for sale and the offering for sale of live or dead birds and of any readily recognisable parts or derivatives of such birds' ('Art. 6(1) Activities')
2(A)	25 Species	May be hunted in the geographical sea and land area of all member states (Art. 7(2)) provided it does not 'not jeopardise conservation efforts' (Art. 7)
2(B)	58 Species	May be hunted only in the member states in respect of which they are indicated (Art. 7(3)) provided it does not 'not jeopardise conservation efforts' (Art. 7)
3(A)	7 Species	'Article 6(1) Activities' are not prohibited, 'provided that the birds have been legally killed or captured or otherwise legally acquired' (Art. 6(3))
3(B)	19 Species	'Article 6(1) Activities' may be allowed by member states, 'provided that the birds have been legally killed or captured or otherwise legally acquired' (Art. 6(3))

It is not sufficient under the Directive to simply pass legislation protecting the species that are listed; there is also a requirement under Article 4 for member states to take 'special conservation measures concerning their habitat in order to ensure their survival and reproduction in their area of distribution' (Art. 4(1)). In *Commission* v *Greece* C-334/04 (which was brought under the old Directive) the ECJ held that Greece had failed to meet its obligations on three grounds:

1. classifying protection areas that were too small;

2. not designating protection areas for some species; and

3. designating protection areas that did not correspond to the location of the protected species.

Habitat and ecosystem

The key statute here is Directive 92/43/EEC on the conservation of natural habitats and of wild flora and fauna ('the Habitats Directive'). This specifically aims to 'contribute towards ensuring bio-diversity through the conservation of natural habitats and of wild fauna and flora in the European territory of the Member States' (Art. 2(1)).

Article 3 calls for the establishment of a 'coherent European ecological network of special areas of conservation', called Natura 2000, which will include all of the protected areas set up under the Birds Directive (79/409/EEC). Article 3 continues that:

Each Member State shall contribute to the creation of Natura 2000 in proportion to the representation within its territory of the natural habitat types and the habitats of species referred to in [Annex I and Annex II]. (Art. 3(2))

Annexes to the Habitats Directive (as amended by Directive 97/62/EC)

Annexe	Coverage
I	Coastal and Halophytic [salty] habitat. 6 types, 28 sub-types
	Costal sand dunes and inland dunes. 3 types, 21 sub-types
	Freshwater habitats. 2 types, 17 sub-types
	Temperate heath and scrub. 9 sub-types
	Sclerophyllus scrub (Matorral) [Mediterranean-type shrubland with evergreen plants with small leathery leaves]. 4 types, 13 sub-types
	Natural and semi-natural grassland formations. 5 types, 25 sub-types
	Raised bogs and mires and fens. 3 types, 12 sub-types
	Rocky habitats and caves. 3 types, 14 sub-types
	Forests. 5 types, 59 sub-types
II	Several hundred species of plants and animals listed

Since 1996, there have been 50 judgments of the ECJ on cases brought by the Commission against member states for failing to meet their obligations under the Habitats Directive (Curia, 2013). To this can be added a further 41 ECJ judgments in cases brought by the Commission against member states for failing to meet their obligations under the 1979 Birds Directive. This is out of a total of around 250 cases coming under the heading of 'environment and consumers' (Curia, 2013). Bell, McGillivray and Pedersen (2013) state that 'habitat conservation law is one of the more contentious areas of Community Environmental Law' (pp. 738–9) and the fact that close to 40 per cent of all environmental cases brought by the Commission in the past 18 years come under these two Directives reinforces that stance.

Morge v *Hampshire CC* [2010] EWCA Civ 150

Concerning: planning; environment; administration of justice

Facts

Hampshire County Council granted planning permission for a bus route along an overgrown disused railway line which had become a habitat for bats and badgers. M argued that this was a breach of Article 12(1)(b) of the Habitats Directive, as the Council had granted planning permission for a bus route which would disturb protected species.

Legal principle

Held that Article 12(1)(b) required member states to prohibit deliberate disturbance of protected species, but that what amounted to disturbance is somewhere between *de minimis* and significant, and that 'the issue is one of degree' (per Sir David Keene) to be decided on a case-by-case basis.

UK law

Historical development

Prior to the start of the nineteenth century, the main emphasis on conservation was in relation to game and hunted species (e.g. deer) with areas in which to hunt them. The New Forest in Dorset, for example, which is now a national park (see below) was 'designated as a Royal Forest and hunting ground by William the Conqueror' in 1079 (New Forest National Park Authority, 2011).

In the nineteenth and early twentieth centuries, in this area as in all environmental law, there was some legislation, but it was reactive and piecemeal. The preamble to the Preservation of Sea Birds Act 1869, for example, states that: 'the sea birds of the United Kingdom have of late years greatly decreased in number; [and] it is expedient therefore to protect their numbers during the breeding season.'

A further drawback was the lack of any official bodies to enforce or even monitor the impact of the scant legislation that was passed. This was left to voluntary organisations, which were also responsible for creating the first protected areas. The Norfolk Naturalist Trust bought Cley Marches in 1926 and the RSPB bought its first reserve at Romney Marsh in 1930. The problem with this common-law approach was that the only protection came from ordinary property rights – animals, birds and plants are subject to the ownership of the landowner, for example, and have protection from trespass and interference by anyone else whilst they are on that land. The reactive nature of common law meant that any damage to property would be compensated, but in the area of nature and conservation that was often an insufficient remedy. The nature conservation value of the RSPB Romney Marsh reserve was destroyed when neighbouring land was drained in 1950, and so it was sold off.

In 1947, the Huxley Committee (aka the Wild Life Conservation Special Committee) issued a report 'Conservation of Nature in England and Wales'. The Report's recommendations were accepted, and the Nature Conservancy Board was set up in 1948. Since then, the administration of nature conservation has undergone many changes, as shown in Figure 10.1, and today Natural England is the responsible body for England.

In the early stages, the scientific basis of nature conservation was emphasised and it was connected firmly to education and research, but Natural England's general purpose was set out by the Natural Environment and Rural Communities Act 2006 as being 'to ensure that the natural environment is conserved, enhanced and managed for the benefit of present and future generations, thereby contributing to sustainable development' (s. 2(1)). Schedule 1 to the Act gives the full details of the constitution of Natural England.

Statute: Flora and fauna

The provisions of the Wildlife and Countryside Act 1981, along with the historical influence of voluntary bodies, results in the strongest legislation being for birds. Section 1 of the Act makes it an offence to deliberately or recklessly 'kill, injure or take any wild bird' or to interfere with its nest or eggs, or to be in possession of a wild bird or its egg, either wholly or in part, alive or dead. The sale or advertising of wild birds is also illegal under s. 6.

Schedule 1 lists 79 rarer species of birds, increasing the penalty to £5,000 – even disturbing such birds or dependent young is an offence.

There are exceptions to the provisions of the Act:

- game birds (except illegal methods of killing them), wild fowl listed, pest species listed may only be killed by owner or occupier;
- killing injured bird where the action is an incidental result of a lawful operation or for crop protection/disease prevention/public health and safety (e.g. H5N1 avian bird flu).

Only animals that are listed in Schedule 5 to the WCA are protected in the same manner as birds. This includes bats, reptiles, amphibians and only the rarest of mammals, fish and butterflies.

Plants only warrant one section (s. 13) under the Wildlife and Countryside Act, but the Act makes it an offence for anyone other than the owner or occupier or other authorised person to intentionally uproot a wild plant, and there is a rebuttable presumption that it was a wild plant.

Figure 10.1

CONSERVATION BODIES IN THE UK

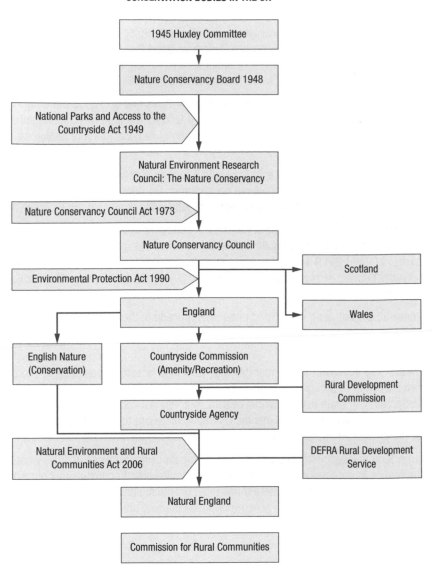

Schedule 8 lists rare wild plants for which picking, uprooting, destroying, sale or advertisement of sale is an offence.

Plants are also included under s. 14 of the Act, which makes it an offence to introduce a non-native species listed in Schedule 9 Part II.

Statute: Habitat

Site of Special Scientific Interest (SSSI)

The SSSI is the most widely used designation of all of the protection areas, and there are over 4,000 in England. Bell McGillivray and Pedersen report that the largest is the Wash at over 600,000 ha, and the smallest 'is a small barn in Gloucestershire notified because it hosts a large breeding colony of lesser horseshoe bats' (2013: 725).

The designation originates under s. 23 of the National Parks and Access to the Countryside Act 1949 and relates to 'any area of land, not being land for the time being managed as a **nature reserve** [that] is of special interest by reason of its flora, fauna or geological or physiographical features'.

The current law concerning SSSIs is in Schedule 9 to the Countryside and Rights of Way Act 2000, but the criteria for designation have not changed. Once Natural England has decided that an area may be special, they must follow the notification period set out in Figure 10.2.

During the notification period, NE specifies what it considers to be 'damaging operations' and these have been interpreted quite widely (see *Sweet* v *Secretary of State for the Environment* [1989] 2 PLR 14), but doing nothing is excluded, as in the case of *R.* v *Nature Conservancy Council, ex parte London Brick Co Ltd* [1996] Env LR 1, where May J said that 'there is no power to compel positive action'.

Even once a SSSI has been designated under this procedure, the process has been described as 'toothless'. In *Southern Water Authority* v *Nature Conservancy Council* (1993) 65 P & CR 55, Mustill LJ said that:

> It needs only a moment to see that this regime is toothless, for it demands no more from the owner or occupier of an SSSI than a little patience. Unless [NE] can convince the Secretary of State that the site is of sufficient national importance to justify an order . . . the owner will within months be free to disregard the notification and carry out the proscribed operations no matter what the cost to the flora, etc. on the site.

SSSIs work on management schemes (s. 28J) and management notices (s. 28K) where the owners remain in possession of the land, but NE is empowered to compulsorily purchase land under s. 28N on occasions where it has been unable to conclude a management scheme or notice, or feels that the scheme or notice is being breached.

Figure 10.2

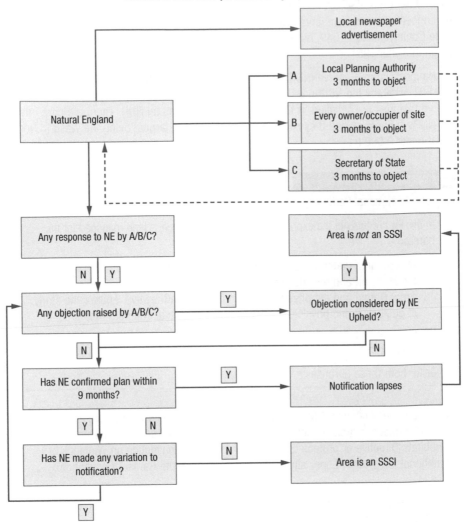

SSSI NOTIFICATION PROCEDURE
Section 28 WCA 1981 (as amended by CROWA 2000)

There is a list of offences in relation to SSSIs contained in s. 28P of the WCA, and they generally carry a maximum £20,000 fine on summary conviction or an unlimited fine if convicted on indictment.

Natural England (July 2013) report that, by area, 96.23 per cent of SSSIs are either in a 'favourable' (37.59 per cent) or 'unfavourable recovering' (58.64 per cent) condition, and this exceeds the Public Service Agreement target of 95 per cent by 2010, but is a slight fall on the equivalent figures for June 2011 (96.64 per cent, 36.59 per cent favourable, 60.05 per cent unfavourable recovering).

National Nature Reserves (NNRs)

The concept of a nature reserve was introduced by s. 15 of the National Parks and Access to the Countryside Act 1949, but the first one (Bienn Eighe in north-west Scotland, was not designated until 1951.

The National Nature Reserve (NNR) was introduced by s. 35 of the Wildlife and Countryside Act 1981, whereby the NCC (now Natural England) could designate any existing nature reserve that they are satisfied 'is of national importance' as an NNR. There are currently 224 NNRs in England, and they cover over 94,000 ha, the largest being the Wash in Norfolk at just under 9,000 ha.

KEY DEFINITION: Nature reserve

Section 15 National Parks and Access to the Countryside Act 1949

In this Part of this Act the expression 'nature reserve' means land managed for the purpose –

(a) of providing, under suitable conditions and control, special opportunities for the study of, and research into, matters relating to the fauna and flora of Great Britain and the physical conditions in which they live, and for the study of geological and physiographical features of special interest in the area, or

(b) of preserving flora, fauna or geological or physiographical features of special interest in the area,

or for both those purposes.

Within a European context, NNRs are very important. A number of sites are also designated as special protection areas under the Birds Directive, special areas of conservation under the Habitats Directive or protected sites under the 1971 Convention on Wetlands of International Importance Especially as Waterfowl Habitat (the Ramsar Convention).

Natural England (in June 2011) report that, by area, 97.64 per cent of NNRs are either in a 'favourable' (52.56 per cent) or 'unfavourable recovering' (45.08 per cent) condition, and this exceeds the Public Service Agreement target of 95 per cent by 2010.

National Parks

As the name suggests, the National Parks and Access to the Countryside Act 1949 is the source of national parks. The power of designation was originally with the National Parks Commission and the criteria for designation under s. 5(2) of the Act are:

(a) their natural beauty, and

(b) the opportunities they afford for open-air recreation, having regard both to their character and to their position in relation to centres of population (s. 5(b)).

The powers, which are now exercised by Natural England, were enhanced by the Natural Environment and Rural Communities Act 2006, which added a new s. 5(2A):

Natural England may –

(a) when applying subsection (2)(a) in relation to an area, take into account its wildlife and cultural heritage, and

(b) when applying subsection (2)(b) in relation to that area, take into account the extent to which it is possible to promote opportunities for the understanding and enjoyment of its special qualities by the public.

There are ten national parks in England, and they are managed by the Council for National Parks. Each of the National Park Authorities acts as its own Planning Authority.

Marine Protected Areas

In England, this designation is a wider one which includes European Marine Sites (essentially the Special Areas of Conservation under the EU Habitats Directive, and Special Protected Areas under the EU Birds Directive which are marine-based), those SSSIs which 'extend into the marine environment below low water mark', Ramsar-designated sites, and Marine Conservation Zones, designated by the Marine and Coastal Access Act 2009.

The MPA will form a network of sites, and will:

promote the recovery and conservation of marine ecosystems. The network will contain MPAs of different sizes containing different habitats and species, connected through movements of adults and larvae, with a range of protection levels that are designed to meet objectives that single MPAs cannot. A well designed network is key to achieving biodiversity goals.' (NE, 2013).

Most of the sites which come under the MPA banner are either SACs or SPAs, and there is only one MCZ, which is based around Lundy Island in the Bristol Channel.

> **□ REVISION NOTE**
>
> National Park Authorities act as Planning Authorities and may cross county boundaries, so think about the implications this may have on planning law, as covered in Chapter 5.

■ Putting it all together

Answer guidelines

See the essay question at the start of the chapter.

Approaching the question

Clearly, this is a question that concerns the a range of measures that have been put into place to regulate and protect biodiversity, so you should start out with introducing the different types of designation that you are going to discuss, as well as how and why they are made. You could also detail the EU measures that triggered some of the designation, although you should of course remember that many of the designations originated in the National Parks and Access to the Countryside Act 1949. Depending on the time available, it will probably not be possible to discuss every single type of classification, so think about which are the most relevant for your answer.

Important points to include

■ Lawton states that 'there is considerable overlap between these designations. For example, 95 per cent of NNRs, 23.5 per cent of National Parks and 11.8 per cent of AONBs are also SSSIs, so working out how much of England is part of the protected area network is a non-trivial exercise' (2011: 3). This quote illustrates the problem outlined in the question well, and you could go into detail about *why* it is important to work out how much of England is part of the protected network, and how this might impact on the effectiveness of biodiversity protection.

■ Give examples of the scale of habitat being important in terms of the UK's obligations under EU schemes such as Natura 2000, for example.

  Make your answer stand out

Link ideas about landscape designation and biodiversity protection to the broader concepts such as sustainability. Pieraccini, for example, argues that the standardisation of lists of operations likely to damage SSSIs are off-putting to owners and occupiers 'and is perceived as unnecessarily constraining their agricultural activities and property rights' (2010: 101), whereas they could be part of a reconciliation of the 'often competing aspects of sustainability' (p. 114).

READ TO IMPRESS

Bell, S., McGillivray, D. and Pedersen, O. (2013) *Environmental Law*, 8th Edn. Oxford: Oxford University Press

Birnie, P., Boyle, A. and Redgwell, C. (2009) *International Law and the Environment*, 3rd Edn. Oxford: Oxford University Press

Curia (2013) Case Law of the Court of Justice, http://curia.europa.eu/jcms/jcms/j_6/

French, D. (2009) Finding autonomy in international environmental law and governance, *J. Env. L.* 21(2), 255–89

Harrop, S. (2011) 'Living in harmony with nature?' Outcomes of the 2010 Nagoya Conference of the Convention on Biological Diversity, *J. Env. L.* 23(1), 117–28

Lawton, J. (2011) Making space for nature, *Env. L. Rev.* 13(1), 1–8

Leakey, R. and Lewin, R. (1996) *The Sixth Extinction: Biodiversity and its Survival*, London: Wiedenfield & Nicholson

Lemieux, A. and Clarke, R. (2009) The international ban on ivory sales and its effects on elephant poaching in Africa, *Brit. J. Criminol.* 49(4), 451–71

NE (2013) http://www.naturalengland.org.uk/ourwork/marine/mpa/default.aspx

New Forest NPA (2011) History of the New Forest, www.newforestnpa.gov.uk/learning-about/history

Norris, K. and Pain, D. (eds) (2002) *Conserving Bird Biodiversity*, Cambridge: Cambridge University Press

Pieraccini, M. (2010) Sustainability and the English commons: a legal pluralist analysis, *Env. L. Rev.* 12(2), 94–114

Pires, S. and Clarke, R. (2011) Sequential foraging, itinerant fences and parrot poaching in Bolivia, *Brit. J. Criminol.* 51(2), 314–35

Secretariat of the Convention on Biological Diversity (2010) *Global Biodiversity Outlook 3*. Montreal

Trouwborst, A. (2009) International nature conservation law and the adaptation of biodiversity to climate change: a mismatch? *J. Env. L.* 21(3), 419–42

www.pearsoned.co.uk/lawexpress

Go online to access more revision support including quizzes to test your knowledge, sample questions with answer guidelines, podcasts you can download, and more!

And finally, before the exam . . .

The most important thing to keep in mind when answering any question on environmental law is that for all of the overlaps with other areas of law, and conceptual problems identified in this guide, a great deal of the law is straightforward. Whether it is an essay question or a problem question, the key is to read it carefully, and make some brief (bullet point) notes on the areas of environmental law that have relevance – and remember, it may be more than one area of environmental law. Once you have that framework, you can fit the main body of your answer within it, and identify to the examiner that you are aware of any overlaps.

Test yourself

- ☐ Look at the **revision checklists** at the start of each chapter. Are you happy that you can now tick them all? If not, go back to the particular chapter and work through the material again. If you are still struggling, seek help from your tutor.

- ☐ Attempt the **sample questions** in each chapter and check your answers against the guidelines provided.

- ☐ Go online to **www.pearsoned.co.uk/lawexpress** for more hands-on revision help and try out these resources:

  - ☐ Try the **test your knowledge** quizzes and see whether you can score full marks for each chapter.

  - ☐ Attempt to answer the **sample questions** for each chapter within the time limit and check your answers against the guidelines provided.

  - ☐ Listen to the **podcast** and then attempt the question it discusses.

  - ☐ **'You be the marker'** and see whether you can spot the strengths and weaknesses of the sample answers.

  - ☐ Use the **flashcards** to test your recall of the legal principles of the key cases and statutes you've revised and the definitions of important terms.

■ Linking it all up

Check where there are overlaps between subject areas. (You may want to review the 'revision note' boxes throughout this text.) Make a careful note of these, as knowing how one topic may lead into another can increase your marks significantly. Here are some examples:

- ✔ The precautionary principle (Chapter 3) overlaps with planning law (Chapter 5) and environmental permitting (Chapter 6).
- ✔ Environmental impact assessments under planning law (Chapter 5) have strong links with IPPC permits and environmental permits (Chapter 6).
- ✔ The laws governing environmental permits (Chapter 6) also have an impact in relation to water pollution (Chapter 8) and waste management (Chapter 9).
- ✔ The industrial emissions element of air pollution (Chapter 7) is now covered by environmental permitting regulations (Chapter 6).
- ✔ The operation of national park authorities (Chapter 10) in relation to planning (Chapter 5).

■ Knowing your cases

Make sure you know how to use relevant case law in your answers. Use the table below to focus your revision of the key cases in each topic. To review the details of these cases, refer back to the particular chapter.

Key case	How to use	Related topics
Chapter 1 – Introduction to environmental law		
Rylands v *Fletcher* (1865) LR 1 Ex 265	This case marked the development of a new area of tort law, and the introduction of 'non-natural' land use	Sources of law
Chapter 2 – Definitions of environmental law		
Customs and Excise Commissioners v *Parkwood Landfill Ltd* [2002] EWCA Civ 1707	To emphasise the importance of the Directive 2008/98 definition of Waste	Waste

Key case	How to use	Related topics
Chapter 3 – Sources and concepts of environmental law		
Commission v *Denmark* 302/86 [1988] ECR 4607	Member states may bypass the rules against discriminatory practices in relation to manufacturing on the grounds of environmental protection	Environmental law and economic tools Sources of law
Öneryildiz v *Turkey* [2004] ECHR 657	To provide a causal link between severe environmental pollution and impact on people's wellbeing. It also illustrates that environmental degradation can contravene Art. 2 of the ECHR	Human rights and the environment
Chapter 4 – Enforcement of environmental law		
R v *HM Inspectorate of Pollution, ex p Greenpeace (No 2)* [1994] Env LR 76	To demonstrate the widening of *locus standi* in judicial review cases, and also to introduce discussions of the level of impact this has had in practice	Introduction to environmental law Role of NGOs in environmental law
Chapter 5 – Planning law		
R (on the application of Prudential Assurance Company Ltd) v *Sunderland City Council* [2010] EWHC 1771 (Admin)	To illustrate that attempts by developers to seek assessment of individual elements of a development scheme rather than the whole scheme are 'artificial'	Enforcement of environmental law
Gateshead MBC v *Secretary of State for the Environment* [1995] Env LR 37	This case clarified for the first time that the planning system must not duplicate statutory controls given to other bodies	Air pollution – enforcement of environmental law
Chapter 6 – Environmental permitting		
Ardley Against Incineration v *Secretary of State for Communities and Local Government* [2011] EWHC 2230 (Admin)	Illustrates the fact that a national regulation which refers to a Directive which had not been transposed into national law could nonetheless be applied	Sources of environmental law Public participation in environmental law

▶

Key case	How to use	Related topics
Chapter 7 – Air pollution		
R (on the application of Air Transport Association of America Inc) v *Secretary of State for Energy and Climate Change* [2012] 2 CMLR 4	To confirm validity of Directive 2008/101/EC and the regulations that were based on it	Sources of environmental law
Chapter 8 – Water pollution		
Alphacell v *Woodward* [1972] AC 824	When discussing 'causing' or 'knowingly permitting' to demonstrate that 'causing' pollution carries no specific legal meaning other than the common-sense meaning	Enforcement of environmental law interpretation
Impress (Worcester) Ltd v *Rees* [1971] 2 All ER 357	To illustrate the impact of *novus actus interveniens* on the chain of causation	Enforcement of environmental law
Environment Agency (formerly National Rivers Authority) v *Empress Car Co (Abertillery) Ltd* [1997] Env LR 227	To introduce the four elements of causation	Enforcement of environmental law
Express Ltd (t/a Express Dairies Distribution) v *Environment Agency* [2003] EWHC 448 (Admin)	To show that the 'emergency' defence in water pollution cases is not absolute, and is interpreted quite strictly	Enforcement of environmental law
Chapter 9 – Waste management		
Palin Granit Oy v *Vehmassalon kansanterveystyön kuntayhtymän hallitus* [2002] Env LR 35	To show that holders need to demonstrate certainty of reuse to avoid items being classed as waste	Definitions

Key case	How to use	Related topics
Chapter 10 – Wildlife conservation and landscape management		
Morge v *Hampshire CC* [2010] EWCA Civ 150	This case shows that unlike in other areas with fixed definitions, 'disturbance' in relation to the Habitats Directive is to be decided on a case-by-case basis	Public participation in environmental law Definitions

■ Sample question

Below is an essay question that incorporates overlapping areas of the law. See whether you can answer this question, drawing upon your knowledge of the whole subject area. Guidelines on answering this question are included at the end of this section.

ESSAY QUESTION

Do the Environmental Permitting (England and Wales) Regulations 2010 effectively reflect extant and emerging principles of environmental law?

Answer guidelines

Approaching the question

This question clearly has the potential to overlap several areas of law. The focus is going to be the Permitting Regulations, which cover many different areas of law themselves, but in addition the question asks you to assess the Permitting Regulations in terms of their application of the concepts of environmental law, both extant (e.g. sustainability, precautionary principle, etc.) and emerging (e.g. the right to a safe and healthy environment). The number of these concepts that you explore, and the depth to which you explore them, will depend upon the length of the essay you have been asked to write, of course.

▶

Important points to include

- Start this question, as with all questions, by setting out the parameters of what you are going to cover. You can't get away from the Permitting Regulations, but you can define the aspects on which you are going to focus – the parts of the regulations dealing with water pollution, for example. You can also make it clear whether you are going to try and address all of the different concepts and principles that exist in environmental law, or just some of them (as a tip, the latter approach is much more realistic, unless it is a very long essay).

- Once you have set out your framework, you can make your way through it logically and methodically, making sure you bring the standard requirements of relevant case law, supporting statute and analysis.

- Finish by reiterating the approach that you took, and make sure you have actually answered the question, rather than just presenting a lot of information.

 Make your answer stand out

For a wide-reaching question such as this, the way to make it stand out is to back up the points you are making with current academic debate. If you are focusing on sustainability, for example, remember to mention that it is not a concrete set of rules, but is open to very wide (and inconsistent) interpretation.

Glossary of terms

The glossary is divided into two parts: *key definitions* and *other useful terms*. The key definitions can be found within the chapter in which they occur as well as in the glossary below. These definitions are the essential terms that you must know and understand in order to prepare for an exam. The additional list of terms provides further definitions of useful terms and phrases which will also help you answer examination and coursework questions effectively. These terms are highlighted in the text as they occur but the definition can only be found here.

▪ Key definitions

Air pollution	(a) . . . the introduction by man, directly or indirectly, of substances or energy into the air resulting in deleterious effects of such a nature as to endanger human health, harm living resources and ecosystems and material property and impair or interfere with amenities and other legitimate uses of the environment, and 'air pollutants' shall be construed accordingly (LRTAP, Art. 1).
Best available technique	Article 2(11) Directive 2010/75/EU:
	Best: most effective in achieving high level of protection of the environment as a whole.
	Techniques: both the technology used and the way in which the installation is designed, built, maintained, operated and decommissioned.
	Available: techniques developed on scale allowing implementation in relevant industrial sector under economically and technically viable conditions, taking into consideration costs/advantages as long as they are reasonably accessible to the operator.

Clean development mechanism	FCCC 2011 (Art. 12): Countries can offset their carbon reduction targets by implementing an emission-reduction project in developing countries.
Compliance notice	Specifies the steps a person needs to undertake to secure that the offence to which the notice relates does not continue or recur.
Development	The carrying out of building, engineering mining or other operations in, on, over or under land or making of any material change in the use of any buildings or other land (s. 55(1) TCPA 1990).
Emissions trading	FCCC 2011 (Art. 17): Countries with emission units to spare – emissions permitted them but not 'used' – can sell this excess capacity to countries that are over their targets. Carbon, for example, is now tracked and traded like any other commodity.
Environment	Section 1(2) Environmental Protection Act 1990: 'The Environment' consists of all, or any of the following media, namely the air, water and land, and the medium of air includes the air within buildings and within other natural or manmade structures above or below ground.
Joint implementation	FCCC 2011 (Art. 6): The equivalent to CDM, but both countries are developed.
Long-range trans-boundary air pollution	(b) . . . air pollution whose physical origin is situated wholly or in part within the area under the national jurisdiction of one State and which has adverse effects in the area under the jurisdiction of another State at such a distance that it is not generally possible to distinguish the contribution of individual emission sources or groups of sources. (LRTAP, Art. 1)
Nature reserve	Section 15 National Parks and Access to the Countryside Act 1949: In this Part of this Act the expression 'nature reserve' means land managed for the purpose – (a) of providing, under suitable conditions and control, special opportunities for the study of, and research into, matters relating to the fauna and flora of Great Britain and the physical conditions in which they live, and for the study of geological and physiographical features of special interest in the area, or (b) of preserving flora, fauna or geological or physiographical features of special interest in the area, or for both those purposes.

Non-natural use	Bingham LJ in *Transco Plc* v *Stockport Metropolitan Borough Council* [2004] 2 AC 1 at 4:

In determining whether a particular use is to be regarded as ordinary the following factors are relevant:

(i)   the extent to which the activity is common, customary or usual;

(ii) the nature and extent of any foreseeable danger to others created by the carrying out of the activity;

(iii) whether the activity is being carried on for profit or the personal gratification of its author;

(iv) whether the person carrying on the activity is doing so out of the exercise of choice or under compulsion;

(v) the extent, if any, of the social utility of the activity.

Polluter pays principle

The principle to be used for allocating costs of pollution prevention and control measures to encourage rational use of scarce environmental resources and to avoid distortion in international trade is the so-called 'polluter pays principle'.

This means that the polluters should bear the expenses of carrying out remediation measures decided by the public authorities (OECD, 1974).

Pollution

Section 1(3) Environmental Protection Act 1990 'Pollution of the Environment means . . .':

pollution of the environment due to the release (into any environmental medium) from any process of substances which are capable of causing harm to man or any other living organisms supported by the environment.

Restoration notice

Specifies the steps a person needs to undertake, and the period in which they must be taken, to secure that the position is, so far as possible, restored to what it would have been if the offence had not been committed.

Rules of statutory interpretation

Literal rule: 'the objective of the court is to discover the intention of Parliament as expressed in the words used in the statute and nothing else' (*Stock* v *Frank Jones (Tipton) Ltd* [1978] 1 All ER 948, per Viscount Dilhorne at 951).

Golden rule: 'the grammatical and ordinary sense of the word is to be adhered to, unless that would lead to some absurdity, or some repugnance or inconsistency' (*John Grey and Others* v *William Pearson and Others* (1857) 6 HL Cas 61, per Wensleydale LJ at 106).

Mischief rule: allows the court to base its interpretation on the 'mischief' which previous statute allowed, but which the current law was brought in to address.

Stop notice
Prohibits a person from carrying on an activity specified in the notice until the person has taken the steps specified in the notice.

Sustainable development
Development that meets the needs of the present without compromising the ability of future generations to meet their own needs. It contains within it two key concepts:

1. the concept of 'needs', in particular the essential needs of the world's poor, to which overriding priority should be given; and

2. the idea of limitations imposed by the state of technology and social organisation on the environment's ability to meet present and future needs.

Waste
Directive 2008/98/EC on Waste, Article 3(a):

'Waste' means any substance or object which the holder discards or intends or is required to discard.

Water discharge activity
A 'water discharge activity' means any of the following –

(a) the discharge or entry to inland freshwaters, coastal waters or relevant territorial waters of any –

    (i) poisonous, noxious or polluting matter,

    (ii) waste matter, or

    (iii) trade effluent or sewage effluent;

(b) the discharge from land through a pipe into the sea outside the seaward limits of relevant territorial waters of any trade effluent or sewage effluent;

(c) the removal from any part of the bottom, channel or bed of any inland freshwaters of a deposit accumulated by reason of any dam, weir or sluice holding back the waters, by causing it to be carried away in suspension in the waters, unless the activity is carried on in the exercise of a power conferred by or under any enactment relating to land drainage, flood prevention or navigation;

(d) the cutting or uprooting of a substantial amount of vegetation in any inland freshwaters or so near to any such waters that it falls into them and failure to take reasonable steps to remove the vegetation from these waters.

(Para. 3, Sch. 21 Environmental Permitting (England and Wales) Regulations 2010/675).

■ Other useful terms

Anthropocentric

In terms of environmental ethics, an anthropocentric view is one which is focused solely or primarily on the human aspect of the environment. Issues are considered in terms of their impact on humans.

Ecocentric

In terms of environmental ethics, an ecocentric view is one which is focused on the environment as a whole. It does not necessarily discount the importance of humans, but places humanity no higher than other species in terms of value.

Ratification

The process by which signatory states to an instrument of international law incorporate it into their own legal system. In the UK, this is generally done through the passage of legislation through Parliament.

Index